BUDDHISM
and the Art
of Psychotherapy

NUMBER FIVE

Carolyn and Ernest Fay Series
in Analytical Psychology
David H. Rosen, General Editor

BUDDHISM
and the Art of
Psychotherapy

Hayao Kawai

Foreword by David H. Rosen

TEXAS A&M UNIVERSITY PRESS
College Station

The paper used in this book meets the minimum requirements
of the American National Standard for Permanence
of Paper for Printed Library Materials, Z39.48-1984.
Binding materials have been chosen for durability.

⊗

Illustrations located in first gallery are courtesy of Iwanami
Shoten, Publishers. Illustrations located in third gallery are
courtesy of Ma Satyam Savita.

Library of Congress Cataloging-in-Publication Data

Kawai, Hayao, 1928–
    Buddhism and the art of psychotherapy / Hayao Kawai ;
foreword by David H. Rosen.
        p.   cm. — (Carolyn and Ernest Fay series in analytical
psychology ; no. 5)
    Includes bibliographical references and index.
    ISBN 0-89096-698-2
    1. Psychotherapy—Religious aspects—Buddhism.
2. Buddhism—Psychology.   I. Title.   II. Series.
BQ4570.P76K38   1996
294.3'375—dc20   95-43421
                                                          CIP

NUMBER FIVE
Carolyn and Ernest Fay Series in Analytical Psychology
David H. Rosen, General Editor

The Carolyn and Ernest Fay edited book series, based initially on the annual Fay Lecture Series in Analytical Psychology, was established to further the ideas of C. G. Jung among students, faculty, therapists, and other citizens and to enhance scholarly activities related to analytical psychology. The Book Series and Lecture Series address topics of importance to the individual and to society. Both series were generously endowed by Carolyn Grant Fay, the founding president of the C. G. Jung Educational Center in Houston, Texas. The series are in part a memorial to her late husband, Ernest Bel Fay. Carolyn Fay has planted a Jungian tree carrying both her name and that of her late husband, which will bear fruitful ideas and stimulate creative works from this time forward. Texas A&M University and all those who come in contact with the growing Fay Jungian tree are extremely grateful to Carolyn Grant Fay for what she has done. The holder of the Frank N. McMillan, Jr. Professorship in Analytical Psychology at Texas A&M functions as the general editor of the Fay Book Series.

Contents

Illustrations

Foreword

The stones at the bottom
Seem to be moving;
Clear water.
— Soseki

The Japanese haiku captures the essence of Hayao Kawai. He is a man of few words, but wise ones. For instance, when I asked Kawai what his topic would be for his Fay Lectures and the related book, he answered, "Nonpersonal psychotherapy." I asked him to explain. Kawai replied, "You people in the West talk about personal, interpersonal, and transpersonal psychotherapy—I'm talking about nonpersonal psychotherapy." Again, I inquired what he meant. At last he answered, "I help my clients to become like a stone." I thought to myself, "This won't work; people won't come to hear Kawai talk about people assuming stonelike qualities." While Kawai eventually broadened his topic into something more comprehensive, the stone theme was important and remains as half of the last lecture, now chapter four of this book, "Personal and Impersonal Relationships in Psychotherapy." The stone had also been important to Jung, from his boyhood on ("Am I the one who is sitting on the stone, or am I the stone on which *he* is sitting?"[1]). Bollingen, Jung's spiritual retreat, built and carved of stone, remains a fitting memorial to him.

Silent flowers
Speak also
To that obedient ear within.
—Onitsura

Silence is a recurring theme in Kawai's book. He tells of returning from Zurich and being silent about Jung for ten to fifteen years because he felt his colleagues and clients would not be receptive to Jung's ideas. Kawai also discloses that he has become increasingly silent in his psychotherapeutic work with clients. Silence clearly relates to stones, flowers, and all of nature. The sacredness of Nature (the pre-Buddhist indigenous Shinto religion) is something that is dear to Kawai's heart and soul. Shintoism (like Taoism, its Chinese counterpart) helped to transform Indian and Chinese Buddhism into its unique Japanese version, Zen Buddhism. Hence, as our text unfolds, we see that initially Kawai, who was disillusioned after World War II, adopted a Western ego (self) position. However, his path of individuation allowed him eventually to hold the Zen Buddhist stance of no ego (no-self). In silence, Kawai ends up creatively containing the opposites, ego/no ego and self/no-self, as he holds to "the true middle."[2]

Kawai came to Los Angeles on a Fulbright Fellowship in 1959, and synchronicity worked one of its wonders. He worked with Bruno Klopfer, a Jungian analyst and a professor at the University of California at Los Angeles, and then he saw J. Marvin Spiegelman in personal analysis. Kawai's first dream was prophetic: he was picking up Hungarian coins with an old Taoist sage engraved on them. The dream symbolizes Kawai's individuation process, which has involved connecting East and West.

In ancient pre-Buddhist Japan, the culture was matriarchal. The main Shinto deity was the Sun Goddess, whereas in most cultures the sun is a masculine god. It is noteworthy that Kawai, in the last phase of his Jungian psychoanalytic training, did his thesis on the Japanese Sun Goddess. In archetypal Japan, light and energy emerged from the dark feminine, much as they did in the Gnostic religion, Taoism, and Jung's psychology (the anima). We could say that Kawai sets his dark yin stone next to Jung's light yang stone and that together they form a whole and provide us with meaning that glows and radiates.

Professor Kawai of Kyoto University, the first Jungian psychoanalyst in Japan, is an ambassador providing us with new understanding derived from the perspective of someone rooted in the East. Although Kawai has authored or edited over fifty books in Japanese, this is only his fourth book to be translated into English. His first book in English, *The Japanese Psyche* (1982), won a national literary award in Japan. Kawai's second book, *The Buddhist Priest Myoe: A Life of Dreams* (1988), is about the dream journal of an extremely devout but simple thirteenth-century monk. His third book, *Dreams, Myths and Fairy Tales in Japan* (1995), is a superb collection of Professor Kawai's Eranos lectures. In addition to being a well-known writer, psychologist, and sandplay therapist, Kawai has a keen sense of humor and plays the flute beautifully. While he was staying at my home during the Fay Lectures, birds would line up on a branch outside his window and listen to him play. Talk about being in tune with nature!

The present volume's first chapter deals with Kawai's personal koan: "Am I a Buddhist and/or a Jungian?" His honest reflections parallel Jung's early skepticism about Buddhism (which synchronistically concerned Japanese or Zen Buddhism)[3] and later his positive regard for Buddha's teachings and the "immense help" and "profound meaning" it gave him.[4] Kawai also shares how, in his work with clients, he has moved from a position of ego curing to one of no-ego healing. In addition, he describes the evolving silence in his work and how integrity-full it feels just to sit with and listen to his clients. It almost sounds as if Kawai is a Zen master or now embodies Taoist sage consciousness. As he puts it, "Being there, absent-minded."

In the second chapter, "The 'Ten Oxherding Pictures'

and Alchemy," Kawai reveals how the individuation process is symbolically and meaningfully revealed in two philosophical and artistic picture series, one Eastern and one Western. Kawai then focuses on an additional set of oxherding pictures, done by a modern Japanese woman, which shows (as does a swan maiden found in the healing spring of an eight-year-old Japanese girl's sandplay therapy) that the feminine is reasserting itself in today's Japanese culture—coming full circle to reunite with the ancient Sun Goddess.

Kawai's third chapter, "What Is I?" stands the concept of the Western ego on its head. It was necessary for me to read Kawai's complicated yet simple analysis of ego a second time before I began to comprehend it. Kawai's view of the ego and the self is grounded in Japanese culture, which holds a view of the ego and the self that is opposite to the Western view. Together the Eastern and Western perspectives make a whole circle; jointly they foster an emerging silence in the center. This intriguing chapter is a major contribution to helping us become more conscious of the other (Eastern) point of view. Only through this type of knowledge could we hope to accept, transcend, and transform our separate perspectives into a harmonious view of the whole, which also can be seen as nothingness or everything (Kawai's concept of the Self).

The last chapter, "Personal and Impersonal Relationships in Psychotherapy," extends the term *psychotherapy* to include sitting in silence and holding contradictions or containing opposites. From a midpoint of stillness, Kawai spirals down and up, zigzagging from side to side—all within a circle of wholeness or nothingness. He describes his clients' complaints and symptoms as koans. Kawai ends up seeing his clients as Zen masters. Most indicative of his being a Shinto (and Taoist) shaman is Kawai's focus on sorrow and love as the bases of mutual healing in psychotherapy, where suffering creates meaning for both individuals. Kawai, ultimately, concludes that true integration of East and West is both possible and impossible. However, one ends up sensing intuitively that Kawai's (like Jung's) glass is half full.

I close with these words from the Buddha: "These four are the foodstuffs, . . . which sustain the creatures that are born, and benefit the creatures that seek rebirth. The first is edible food, coarse or fine; touch is second; the thinking capacity of the mind is the third; and the fourth is consciousness."[5]

In the spirit of Buddha, Kawai has given us much "food for thought"—new psychological food from Japan. It will take us a long time to digest it and to derive the needed nourishment from this Eastern offering. Kawai has "touched" us with his own moving and inspiring stories and with those of his clients. He has stretched our "thinking capacity" to new depths and heights. Finally, our "consciousness" has been expanded to the realms of wholeness and nothingness. I bow to Kawai:

All around
That meets the eye
Is cool and fresh.
—Basho

David H. Rosen
College Station, Texas

BUDDHISM
and the Art
of Psychotherapy

Prologue

In psychotherapy, it is important that the patient be able to attain a proper psychic state, in which the conscious and the unconscious are in harmony. In modern Europe, people have succeeded in establishing a strong ego; this is, as Erich Neumann says, "the peculiar achievement of Western man."[1] This strong ego, although it has attained rich results via scientific knowledge, always is in danger of losing contact with the unconscious. Many patients today are suffering from a "loss of relatedness." In order to recover, the patient should try to investigate her or his own unconscious, as depth psychologists claim to do.

In addition, we must, I think, examine varieties of ego-consciousness. The modern Western ego has accomplished so many things that other cultures all over the world have been strongly influenced by it. However, in view of the fact that the strong modern ego tends to lose contact with the unconscious, it may be worthwhile to investigate ego-consciousness in different cultures. As a Japanese, I would like to talk about the situation in my country.

At the party the evening before the initial Fay Lecture, I began my speech with the following statement: "It is said that a Japanese speaker, on this kind of occasion, tends to begin with apologies, whereas an American likes to begin with a joke. If I am a typical Japanese person, I have to begin by saying that I am not qualified to be a lecturer here and have no knowledge that allows me to talk about psychotherapy." I wondered why this difference exists and got the following interpretation. When people in Japan gather in one place, they share a feeling of unity, regardless of whether they have known each other before or not. One should not stand alone, separated from others. Therefore, when one becomes a speaker, one has to apologize, asserting that one is no way different from others. In the West, however, even though people come together in one place, each person is separate from the others, as an individual. Therefore, when one becomes a speaker, he or she likes to begin with a joke, enabling all the people there, by laughing together, to experience a feeling of oneness.

This example suggests the difference between the ego-consciousness of the Japanese and that of Westerners. In the West, a person tries to establish an individual ego separate from others and then tries to find ways to have relationships with others. In contrast, a Japanese person seems to establish a feeling of oneness first and then tries to become an individual separate from others.

Looking at things from a particular culture's viewpoint, it is easy to criticize a different cultural group; but in fact it is impossible to judge which of two stances is "right." In seeking a postmodern consciousness, we can, I think, come to know each other and, to our benefit, find something new.

Investigating Japanese consciousness, I found a strong influence from Buddhism. In my own practice of psychotherapy, I was not aware of it for some time. However, when I had opportunities to talk in the United States and Europe about my practice, I gradually became cognizant of the importance of Buddhism in my psychotherapy. Western observers helped me become conscious of my way of practicing.

It is a remarkable fact that, early in 1939, C. G. Jung noticed the importance of Zen and remarked in his foreword to

Suzuki's *Introduction to Zen Buddhism:* "This tells us a good deal about the 'content of enlightenment.' The occurrence of satori is interpreted and formulated as a breakthrough, by a consciousness limited to the ego-form, into the non-ego-like self. This view is in accord not only with the essence of Zen, but also with the mysticism of Meister Eckhart."[2] Thus he grasped the essence of Zen, but he was hesitant to introduce it directly to the West. He said, "A direct transplantation of Zen to our Western conditions is neither commendable nor even possible."[3] It must have been true at that time. Is it now? That is not a simple question to answer. However, even if I should agree with Jung, in a sense, that "a direct transplantation" is not possible, I think, as I mentioned above, that mutual learning is meaningful.

I, an Oriental, learned a great deal from Jung's psychology. To recount my personal experience—how a Japanese became a Jungian analyst, and how Buddhism in him gradually reacted to it—might be worthwhile, not only for Japanese readers but also for Western ones.

Chapter 1

Buddhist? Jungian?
What Am I?

Since my return from Zurich, Switzerland, in 1965, I have practiced as a Jungian analyst in Japan. During the past thirty years, while working with many clinical cases, I have been introducing Jung's psychology and organizing Jungian training and education. Now, with thirteen Japanese analysts practicing here, it is evident that this effort has been fruitful.

I have quite naturally thought of myself as a Jungian analyst all this time and never have thought seriously of myself as a Buddhist. Nor have I thought that I might be practicing psychotherapy based on Buddhist principles. However, when I attempted recently to present an integrated overview of my method of practicing psychotherapy to Westerners, I was astonished to uncover some deeply embedded Buddhist elements. Therefore, in this book I would like to focus on what I have discovered about my own relationship to Buddhism.

I must make it clear that I have no intention of writing about psychotherapy based upon Buddhist ideas or of comparing Jung's theories with Buddhist cosmology. There are many who are better qualified to write on those subjects.[1] During the time when "I," an individual, underwent Jungian training and then devoted myself to practicing and teaching Jungian analysis in this "foreign" Japanese culture, this "I" underwent conscious and unconscious transformations. My purpose then, in writing this book, is to review my method of psycho-therapy and to take a fresh look at this "I" in its relation to Buddhism.

Daring to publish such ramblings in English may be of little use except in considering the adaptations one must make when shifting certain materials from one culture to an-other. This subject, however, does relate deeply to basic issues concerning the methodology of my psychotherapy research. It is this aspect which I feel may be of interest to my readers.

1. From Individual to Universal

Both Freud and Jung insisted that their psychotherapies were "science." Given the circumstances of their time, it was nec-essary to declare that their work was science in order to get their newly created methods recognized by society. And, in-deed, they themselves viewed psychotherapy as fundamen-tally science, since it was a system based not upon speculation but upon practical experience. Furthermore, in applying the method to patients and getting practical results from it, they thought that they were getting acceptable proof of its scien-tific nature. But when you look at it from today's perspective, the shakiness of its status as science becomes obvious.

The fact that there are various schools of thought in depth psychology itself would make a natural scientist— whose viewpoint is that there is one truth—uncomfortable.[2] When certain phenomena occur, depth psychology may in-terpret or explain them in hindsight, but it cannot pre-dict phenomena with anything like the degree of accuracy achieved by the natural sciences. I need not say more on this, since it has become clearer to us that psychotherapy—espe-cially that based on depth psychology—is not, and should not be, considered in the same manner as natural science.

In particular, I would like to discuss here differences in methodology. According to modern natural science, there is a clear distinction between the observer and the phenomenon being observed. Because of that, the results of such observation are considered to have "universal validity," since anyone can become a like observer. From the beginning, however, Freud's and Jung's research grew out of their own self-analyses. Both these men established their theoretical systems and their methods upon the foundation of their own experience of self-analysis, which they largely performed on themselves as they recovered from psychic illness. Ellenberger has called this sort of ailment called "creative illness."[3]

These pioneering analysts objectified their personal experience as far as possible, trying to reach universal conclusions, so that their theories could receive broad understanding, approval, and application. But, insofar as the observer becomes deeply involved in his own phenomena, the situation differs completely from the ideal of modern natural science.

Why, then, is such an "unscientific" procedure needed? I hear people who come for psychotherapy asking such questions as "Why did my mother die when I was three years old?" To such a question, natural science answers: "Because your mother got tuberculosis," "Many people died of TB around that time," or "There was no medicine for TB then." But the questioner never is satisfied with such answers. What this person wants to know is: "Why did my mother have to die when I was only three, leaving me alone?" It is the relation of such a phenomenon to one's own self that one seeks to grasp. Natural science studies an individual and a phenomenon separately. This person, though, is demanding an answer concerning the individual's relation to the phenomenon. For the therapist to respond to this question appropriately, it becomes necessary to develop an understanding of the phenomenon which strictly validates its relationship to the individual.

In modern times, the rapid development of our natural sciences and technology has made it possible for us human beings to control or manipulate manifold objects and conditions and thus to realize many of our own desires. Seeing the extent to which this has proceeded, I suspect that we humans have developed too much confidence in ourselves and our interests. We assume that now we can or should get anything we want, and we don't hesitate willfully to try to manipulate any object. We tend to think that we can understand anything through our scientific knowledge and to assume that nearly anything is possible. Since the split separating object and self underlies our scientific thinking and we overutilize the intellect for everything, we cannot help but fall victim to the illness called "loss of relatedness." Virtually anyone who comes to a psychotherapist suffers some degree of this "loss of relatedness."

It was in response to this illness that Freud and Jung sought to develop a mentality which presupposed "relatedness." Through their own healing processes, as they overcame their respective illnesses, they worked on connecting the *ego* to the whole *Self*. As they did this, they tried to realize "universal knowledge." That is to say, they explored the path going "from individual to universal." This path was entirely different from the paths followed by the natural sciences toward the universal, which ignore or negate the person.

From the foregoing, you will understand why it is not nearly as easy to apply the theories of depth psychology to human beings as it is to apply physics theories to objects. It is possible for a psychoanalyst, guided by the theories of depth psychology, to help an analysand to start from her/his self and then, in relation to that, to explore the inner and outer worlds. However, it is not possible to "apply" the theory while ignoring or denying the analysand's presence or being as an individual. No matter what one's school of depth psychology was, if one believed simply in "science," one would fail in the application of such a theory.

Speaking out of my own personal experience, as I have come to understand the nature of knowledge in depth psychology, I believe that awareness of the connection of the individual to the universality has great meaning to many people. Especially in order to understand what Jung called the *Collective Unconscious*, I think that one must open oneself to the experiences of people in various cultures and try to incorporate such experiences in one's whole world view. Jung himself showed deep understanding of non-European cultures, despite a rather strong trend toward Eurocentric thought during his time.

Rather than venture into Buddhist doctrine or into psychotherapy from a Buddhist perspective, I shall discuss, primarily out of my own experience, the role Buddhism played while I was practicing analysis in Japan as an individual very much on my own, spending lots of time wondering, getting lost, wandering.

2. Buddhism and I

When I became a Jungian analyst, I found it virtually unthinkable that I ever would become deeply interested in Buddhism. I had been vaguely rejecting Buddhism since my childhood. It seemed like something rather ominous, even sinister. Most Japanese are "Buddhist"—i.e., born into Buddhist families—but we don't feel obliged to attend weekly ceremonies or sermons by our priests, in the way Christians attend church. I would say that, unless there is a funeral for a family member, we have little occasion to become aware of actually being Buddhist.

When I entered the United States the first time, there was a space on one of the forms for "your religion." I remember even now writing "Buddhism" with great hesitation. Some Japanese wrote "None." Because of that, those people were assumed to be "atheists" in the Western sense. This assumption caused considerable misunderstanding, because at that time "atheist" often was equated with "Communist." Later I shall discuss how this sort of misunderstanding could occur, due to the fact that Japanese spirituality is not necessarily tied to specific religions. Like other Japanese, I was an "unaware Buddhist."

I believe that my negative reaction to Buddhism stemmed from the following. My younger brother died when I was four years old. As his coffin was taken out, I cried and clung to the coffin, exclaiming, "Don't throw this away!" My mother, of course, suffered deep shock from my brother's death. She wept and kept chanting in front of our Buddhist shrine. I must have stayed beside my mother in grief. As I grew older, my mother often told me about these things. Having listened to this story so many times, I thought that I had my own memory of it, but the latter may simply be images I formed afterwards. Because of such an experience in childhood, Buddhism and chanting seem to have provoked, as I was growing up, anxiety and fear relating to death. I clearly remember having a great fear of death rather early on. In the year following my brother's death, I can remember holding my breath, closing my eyes, and thinking to myself, "Death must be like this" or "You lose all your senses and don't know anything." I was fascinated by the thoughts generated by this fear. Buddhism didn't seem in the least able to rescue me from death; rather, it made me all too conscious of death and my strong connection to it. So, under these ominous circumstances, the distance between myself and Buddhism grew. I knew only that our family belonged to the Jodo (Pure Land) sect, but I had no desire to know about its founder, Honen, or his teachings.

My father impressed me deeply. He loved Zen sayings.

日 日 是 好 日

[Each day is a fine day] was his favorite.
I also remember,

直指人心　見性成仏

[Truly focusing on oneself, one realizes Buddhahood.]

Many times I heard from him the story of Bodhi Dharma's "sitting for nine years, facing the wall." Since I respected him so, I thought that he must have been enlightened, perhaps especially because he had no fear of death, which was such a terrible problem for me.

When I grew up, I hoped that I would reach enlightenment. Although I did not know the "reality" of Zen, this hope gained great importance in my mind. I was strongly attracted by the understanding that, through "enlightenment," all anxiety and fear would dissolve at once.

World War II broke out when I reached adolescence. As the Japanese military gained strength, the ideal of boys becoming soldiers and dying for our country became part of our indoctrination in the schools. While intellectuals in the cities were resistant to such ideas, people in the countryside where I lived tended to adopt that attitude. The terrible thing for me was that my fear of death was not decreasing at all. I didn't want to die, and I disliked the idea of killing others. Therefore, I was not capable of even wanting to become a soldier. Being such a "total coward," I could not even talk about my view to anyone: "I'm sorry, but since I'm scared to die, I can't become a soldier!"

I watched my classmates in junior high with respect when they said they would die for our country and subsequently entered army and navy schools.

I did not have any such desire and was troubled by this weakness. Finally, I wrote a letter to my eldest brother, who was in medical school at that time: "What shall I do? I feel ashamed that I am scared to die and therefore don't want to become a soldier. I see that both you and Father are enlightened about death because you studied medicine. I don't like medicine, but I am considering medical school. What do you think about this?"

His response came immediately:

> Fear of death is natural. You don't need to feel ashamed. Devotion to our country is not limited to becoming a soldier. You will become useful for our country only when you do what you like to do.
>
> If you study medicine, you will understand death of the body, but still you won't know what death means to man. It will take your whole life to find that out. There is no one

particular sort of study which is better than others to prepare for this. Regarding death, Father and I both are not enlightened at all. So don't worry. Take your time to think about all this, while you do what you like to do.

The most impressive part of his letter to me was his clear statement: "Both Father and I are not enlightened at all." Even my father, who appeared to be unshakable and fearless, was not enlightened. And, when I read that death is the problem which requires lifelong search, my feeling of cowardly shame suddenly lifted and disappeared. And what he said about fear was also true. Even now at my age, not having experienced enlightenment, I still fear dying. One thing which has not changed since that time is that death remains my lifelong question.

Eventually, direct contact with Buddhism occurred unexpectedly. It didn't happen until I went abroad to study in the United States. In order to encounter my native Eastern religion, I had to travel to the West, first to the United States and then to Switzerland. The "Ten Oxherding Pictures" and the mandala I discuss later were introduced to me for the first time in the United States, through my first analyst, Dr. Marvin Spiegelman. I was enchanted by them, but quite frankly also somewhat mystified, if not actually suspicious. In this manner, America gave me a chance to begin to connect with Buddhism.

3. Longing for the Western World

Before exploring my deepening relation to Buddhism, I would like to discuss why I went abroad to study. In my childhood, as the military increased in power, the movement sweeping the whole nation into war grew stronger. Unfortunately, Japanese mythology was used by the military to bolster their slogan: "Japan is the Divine Nation; thus she will never be defeated." I accepted this naively, just as I was taught. But, since I had the tendency to think rationally, I, unlike my peers, thought that something was wrong about this, and from time to time I suffered over it alone.

As the U.S. Army attacks became more and more severe, a certain great soldier one day visited our junior high school and gave a speech. He said that, looking over our long history, we can see that the invaders will have victory for a short time, but eventually they will be defeated. Thus the U.S. Army now trying to invade Japan will soon lose the war.

Listening to this lecture, I could agree with the first half of his argument. But then, as I thought a little, I realized that, in fact, Japan had invaded first. So, I concluded, Japan will lose in the end. This terrible thought devastated me. Shaken by such a thought of my own, I tried to deny it. I sought to chase away such an ominous idea. But the more I tried, the stronger it grew in my mind. People around me all believed in our victory. I suffered unbearably by myself with my different belief. It was so bad that finally I confided in one of my brothers, hoping that he would show me some evidence, anything, that would indicate that my idea was wrong. But my brother neither denied nor supported my view. Instead he just strictly forbade me to tell anyone, even my parents.

Japan was defeated when I was seventeen. After the war, it gradually became obvious how irrational had been the arguments that we had been taught. Since I already had entertained such ideas, I was ready to accept Western rationalism totally. In addition, I was left with a strong prejudice against Japanese mythology. Thus, with very few exceptions, I strongly rejected all things Japanese. I felt an attraction toward Western accomplishments such as literature and art. I liked virtually everything Western, while Japanese things seemed irrational to me. They seemed to pull me down into darkness when I was trying to get the blessing of sunlight into my life.

I thought that, for Japan to recover from her defeat, the most important thing was for her to learn from modern Western rationalism. For that reason I thought that I should study science, so I majored in mathematics at my university and became a high school math teacher. I was close to embracing science as almighty. From this perspective, I looked down on Buddhist teaching as hardly worth anyone's attention.

Indeed, lots of young people tried to think in a rational way. Many were attracted to materialism and became Communists, although I did not go in that direction. It sounds strange, but I had a hunch that science-ism was deceptive. Luckily, I followed this hunch. At that time, if you were an intellectual, the trend was toward some degree of materialism. That was considered the "correct" way. But I no longer hesitated to think differently about what others around me were thinking was right.

As a high school teacher, I devoted a lot of energy to education, feeling that this was my vocation. Gradually, however, some and then more and more students began coming to me to talk about their problems. Trying to respond to this need responsibly, I entered a graduate course in clinical psychology at Kyoto University. I soon found that at that time there were no adequate courses or teachers for this subject in Japan. Even so, I continued to study what clinical psychology I could and at my school began to focus more on counseling than on mathematics. Eventually resigning from my position at the high school, I devoted more time to this study and began to lecture on clinical psychology at the university. Ultimately, however, I realized that I had to go to the United States for additional study.

Luckily, I passed the examination for a Fulbright Fellowship. I became a graduate student in psychology at the University of California at Los Angeles (UCLA) in 1959. There I began my serious study of clinical psychology. I was studying the Rorschach technique when I met Dr. Bruno Klopfer at UCLA. He was a Jungian analyst and so, when I became attracted to Jung's ideas, I was introduced to Jungian analysis. In other words, I did not arrive in the United States already familiar with Jung and wanting to study about him. I was led to Jung seemingly by chance, without having known of his ideas.

4. Jungian Analysis

At the beginning of my analysis, I was very surprised to hear the analyst, Dr. Spiegelman, say that we were going to do dream analysis. I immediately protested, saying, "I cannot trust such an irrational thing!" How could I believe in "dream messages" when I came here to study Western rationalism? I asked him. I simply could not believe anything so unscientific.

My analyst responded, "Have you ever studied your dreams—what they mean?"

"No," I answered.

"Don't you think it's rather unscientific to disparage their study when you have not even inspected your dreams?"

I thought that that made sense. I decided to try it, anyway, so I promised to write down my dreams, even though I was skeptical. I had quite an impressive initial dream. I did not understand its meaning at all, but I was surprised to have a dream which had an interesting story line. Then, as I was talking to my analyst about my associations with the dream, I started to get a sense of it. And that was another surprise.

In the dream, I picked up many Hungarian coins. These coins had the design of an old Taoist sage on them. Given my associations to Hungary, the dream seemed to suggest that, to me, Hungary was a bridge to East and West. My analyst said that, to judge from this dream, I eventually might gain insights of great value for the relation between East and West. When I reflect on the course of my life, I recognize that what my analyst surmised indeed has been realized.

After this initial dream, other meaningful dreams followed. I was strongly attracted to these dreams, while still complaining about their "unscientific nature" and expressing dissatisfaction over the "mysticism" in Jungian psychology.

Luckily, my analyst did not get upset with me. He argued with me honestly in every session. Through this exchange, gradually I was able to think through the relation of Jungian psychology and natural science in my own way and thus came to accept this psychology.

It was while studying in Los Angeles that I happened to come into contact with Buddhism again. One day during my analytic session, the analyst showed me the "Ten Oxherding Pictures" from the Zen tradition. What a shame that I had never even known that such pictures existed in the East! As I have mentioned, because of my father's influence, I felt less negative about Zen than about other forms of Buddhism. This was especially true since I had a strong interest in "instant enlightenment." So I was impressed that, in these pictures, the state of enlightenment was depicted as actually being a process. Although this was a rather shallow understanding, my interest in these ten pictures has never faded.

In 1982, I published a critical review of a comparative study of the alchemical pictures in the *Rosarium Philosophorum*, which Jung had commented on, and the "Ten Oxherding Pictures."[4] This was my first attempt at writing an essay relating to Buddhism.

At a party attended by people involved in Jung's work, someone who had expressed an interest in Zen asked me if I had ever read Eugen Herrigel's *Zen and the Art of Archery*.[5] In fact, the book had made a strong impression on me. Herrigel's devotion to understanding Japanese culture, which seemed so foreign to him as a Westerner, had moved me deeply. Later, after I returned to Japan, I read this book again and subsequently used it as a reference.

My interest in Zen increased. I was stimulated by Jung's foreword to D. T. Suzuki's *Introduction to Zen Buddhism*,[6] which I read in English. In this way, I gradually was drawn toward Zen. While I frequently thought that it made sense, I honestly felt that its ideal was virtually unrealizable. A state of enlightenment might exist, but I thought that I never would be able to experience it, nor did I imagine that by Zen practice I might be able to increase my ability as a psycho-therapist.

It is true that, when getting close to someone, even a great man, you start to see his shadow side. Living in Japan, you sometimes see or hear about a "great Zen master." But when you find out that, even after he reaches "enlighten-ment," his selfish aspect, for example, remains as great as be-fore, it makes you wonder. This relates to a fact that I became quite familiar with: no matter how much analysis you receive, your basic personality may not change. So this situation is not peculiar to Zen.

After completing a year and a half of study in Los Angeles, I returned to Japan and from there left for Zurich, where I began study at the C. G. Jung Institute. Since I al-ready had been in analysis, I got into dream analysis right away. In this process I was able to regain contact with my own culture. For example, my interest turned to Japanese literary classics, which I had virtually abandoned. I also read Japanese fairy tales, legends, and myths—all of which helped me re-cover my own roots.

Because my rejection of all things Japanese had been so strong, it was a deep shock to discover through dream analysis that Japanese mythology had great meaning to me. This real-ization was supported by dream "messages" which appeared repeatedly in different forms as my analyst, C. A. Meier, probed: "Isn't it natural to arrive at a Japanese myth when a Japanese person is seeking his roots?" So, finally, I had to wrestle with Japanese myth itself.

Before describing a dream which marked a turning point for me, you need to know that at that time I had two analysts, a man and a woman. But since I had been raised in the Japa-nese tradition of "the man, honored; the woman, subordi-nated," I felt somewhat uneasy receiving analysis from a woman. I felt a resistance to acknowledging a woman as su-perior to me, a man. Presently, my female analyst, Lilian Frey, appeared in my dream. As she approached me, she was enve-loped by light. Awestruck, I knelt down.

I woke up thinking, "She was the Sun!" With this dream, I was given an opportunity, and my attitude toward Ms. Frey began changing. Indeed, my ideas about and attitude toward women in general changed.

Reporting the dream to Ms. Frey, I told her about my feeling toward women in general and told her that this dream had given me a chance to change, and that it had seemed to work. "You were the Sun Goddess, weren't you?" I remarked, explaining that in Japanese mythology, Amaterasu, the Sun Goddess, is most important. You might say she is at least the most prominent figure. Ms. Frey responded, smiling, "I am not a goddess nor the sun. I'm simply a human being. That sun goddess exists in you," she added.

My response to all this was two separate feelings. One side of me felt that this seemed somewhat significant, and the other side felt that it was unacceptable because, at that time, I still had a strong negative feeling toward Japanese mythology.

After accumulating such experiences, I finally dealt with Japanese myths in my final thesis for certification at the institute. My presentation focused on the Sun Goddess, Amaterasu.

Through those rich experiences of analysis, I was able to create, as a Japanese, a foundation to live upon. However, at this time I was not aware of Buddhism as being in any way relevant to my work.

5. Western Consciousness

One day, after studying awhile at the Jung Institute, I had an informal conversation with Dr. Marie-Louise von Franz. She may have been interested in me, since I was the first student from Japan at the institute. Perhaps she was trying to encourage me. She said jokingly, "Coming from far away, you are amazed that we all talk about the unconscious day in and day out, aren't you?"

I replied, "I am not surprised about the unconscious. I feel like I was familiar with it before I got here. But what I am amazed about is the Western consciousness." Dr. von Franz seemed to understand what I meant. "Is that so!" she laughed with delight. Actually, I had collided with the Western consciousness in the United States and again in Europe. It deeply "culture-shocked" me. It is rather threatening for a Japanese to encounter the Western ego, which is developed as an independent entity, as if utterly distinct from all that is not "I" (i.e., everything else). The Japanese presuppose a connection—with others, with all else, in the sense of oneness. They develop the ego without severing that tie. When you notice this difference without being aware of why it is, you will have misunderstandings even in daily conversation or in the basic feel of relationships. To put it abstractly, the Western ego clearly has a strong "cutting" function, separating everything. On the contrary, the Japanese ego has bearing strength, "containing" without "cutting." I could give countless examples, but, here is one example from my own experience.

When I was in analysis in Los Angeles, my fee was considerably reduced by my analyst, since I was a poor foreign student. While I was pleased by such consideration, I had to think about it a great deal, in the following vein: Analysis is the most important matter for me. Although my fee was lowered, is it permissible for me to use that money for recreation? Rather, I should pay the proper fee even at the cost of grocery money. Finally I couldn't stand it any longer and had to tell the analyst my thought. He was surprised and said, "I have considered your financial situation and mine and decided on that fee as reasonable. I have no problem with that. I don't mind at all. Why do you mind? Why do you worry about it when I, the receiver, do not mind at all?"

It was very clear logic. But I felt that something important was getting lost. "I think you are reasonable, but I can't settle it like this. I will think about it for a week," I replied.

The next week I said to him, "I understand your feeling. I will receive your kindness and pay only the reduced fee. However, I can't agree with your idea that, just because you don't mind it, I don't need to worry. Yet, since you have been so generous in this regard, I would like to keep it well in mind so that your good deed is carried on." And, I might add here, his good deed is still affecting my work today.

I wonder if this example indicates to you the difference between the American attitude of clear-cut logical and also individualized thinking, and the Japanese attitude of relatedness, in which the one side cannot make a proposal without considering the ramifications for the other.

In terms of my understanding of Western consciousness, Erich Neumann's book, *The Origin and History of Consciousness*,[7] had quite an impact on me. It made me realize what a rare achievement the Western ego has become in the world history of the mind. To Neumann, it was obvious that the Japanese never achieved what he called the symbolic "killing of the mother." In his theory, ego development proceeds by stages, and the Japanese ego gets stuck at quite an immature level. This reminded me of what General MacArthur, as commander of the occupying American Armed Forces, said when he left Japan: The Japanese people's mental age is that of a twelve-year-old. It seemed to fit in some way, but certainly I could not agree fully.

After I returned to Japan, I gradually developed my own ideas about the Japanese ego. In comparison with it, I can acknowledge the power of the modern Western ego. The latter is one of many ways of being conscious, but it cannot be said that this is the only correct way. To support this point, it is useful to depict various modes of the ego concretely and compare them with the Western one. I must say that I have spent thirty years doing just this, so I will be discussing the Japanese ego especially in relation to Buddhism.

I would like to tell you of an unintentional confrontation I had with Western consciousness, one which influenced my way of being a Jungian analyst later on. The final examination for certification at the Jung Institute included an oral examination covering various fields. During it, one of the examiners asked me, "What are examples of symbols of the Self?" I should have said, "The mandala" or something equally standard. But at that moment, the Japanese words,

草木国土悉皆成仏

[literally: grass, tree, country, land—completely, all—
become, Buddha],
came to mind. So, I answered spontaneously, "Everything!"
Consequently, the rest of the interchange turned into a
heated discussion. After it was over, that examiner said that
I lacked the basic knowledge of analytical psychology, an understandable conclusion. Various difficulties followed, but
somehow I eventually was able to pass certification.

When I think of how I answered that question and how
hard I insisted on my point in the ensuing discussion, I feel
that there were numerous factors in the background. One of
them, I believe, was an idea which Japanese Buddhism
emphasizes:

森羅万象

[all created things].
Of course, I didn't actually have this phrase consciously avail-
able from my background while defending my statement.
Strictly speaking, according to this Buddhist idea, the "everything" which I affirmed was most assuredly Self-itself. There
is no concept of a symbol of Self. It's just Self. This is important to consider and will be discussed in detail.

This examination given by the Jung Institute was a
deeply meaningful experience. Not only was the candidate
examined as to whether he had knowledge or not, but also
it drew out something of the examinee's being. This "trial"
therefore functioned as an initiation rite for my becoming a
Japanese Jungian.

6. Jungian Analysis in Japan
As soon as I returned home from Switzerland in 1965, I decided to begin practicing psychotherapy, despite the fact that

such therapy was not known to the general public. This lack necessitated a great deal of caution and consideration on my part. Had I spoken carelessly about dream analysis, for instance, people would have seen psychotherapy simply as superstition. Again, regarding the mechanics of therapy, if a Japanese were to go to someone to talk about a problem, not only was the time limited, but they had to pay the fee for just talk. This was unthinkable! Payment was made only for something solid and tangible. Such was the tenor of the time. Japanese intellectuals were too eager to catch up with Western modernization, so they got caught in such a narrow understanding of "scientific nature" that they tended to attack clinical psychology and psychotherapy in general as "unscientific."

I had to remain silent for ten years before I could present my ideas on fairy tales in public, fifteen years for those on myths. During those years, I gradually and carefully introduced dream analysis, first to groups of professionals and much later to the public. This is the sort of caution I exercised initially.

My first patient was a thirteen-year-old boy who had been suffering from school phobia. In his third session, he brought an impressive dream: "I was walking in a field with clover that was taller than me. Then there was a large spiral or whirlpool of flesh. I was almost pulled into it. I woke up in terror."

This dream impressed him as well as me. The spiral has two aspects, one regenerating and the other devouring. Since ancient times, it has often been used as a symbol of the Great Mother archetype. The Earth Mother goddess figurines of ancient Japan have spiral designs incised on them. This dream indicates powerfully how powerless this boy felt when he was exposed to this devouring Great Mother.

When he first told me this dream, I remembered two incidents that had happened upon my return to Japan. It was unusual to take one's family when one went abroad to study at that time, so my parents and relatives threw a great "Welcome Home" party for me. It was customary in Japan to have a sea bream dish for special celebrations, so a beautiful sea bream graced the center of the table. However, when my mother ate some of it, a bone got stuck in her throat. She suffered so much that subsequently she had to go see her doctor many times. Then, at the end of the party, as I was seeing my mother off, I almost smashed her arm with the taxi door.

These two incidents dogged my mind. I was perplexed as to why they had happened. I didn't seem particularly to have hidden or subconscious hostility toward my mother. Then, when I heard this boy's dream, I recognized intuitively that there was a negative Great Mother constellation all over Japan. Not only he, but all of Japan—including me, of course—is under the sway of the Great Mother. I think one of her manifestations is the school-phobia epidemic. Recently there has been a great increase in the number of children who refuse to go to school in Japan. In order to explain such a phenomenon, you must have multiple psychological elements and types. One possibility may be that, as the Great Mother archetype is so strong in Japan, children both want to be with their mother and to be against her. By staying home from school, they can be with the mother physically and, at the same time, rebel against her—as, naturally, she wants them to attend school. In comparing Japanese culture with Western ones, it is useful to look at the degree of dominance of the maternal or the paternal principle.

Practicing analysis in Japan, I thought it was important to consider the dominant power of the mother archetype. Then various Japanese phenomena become understandable. For example, many clients make telephone calls to the therapist outside of the appointment hour or even in the middle of the night. The dependency of clients upon therapists becomes very heavy. Some clients develop the expectation that the therapist will be a Great Mother who can hold anything, accept everything, endlessly. If you are not aware of this but simply try to establish a textbook "contractual relationship" with the client, the client will feel that the therapist is cold, and the therapeutic relationship will be destroyed. The therapist has to recognize that often the Great Mother archetype will be projected onto her or him by the client.

When introducing analytical psychology to the Japanese, I was wondering how to describe an archetype. I soon got the idea that if you begin with a story relating to the Great Mother, people understand. As long as you are Japanese, you are deeply influenced by the Great Mother. Therefore, it is convenient to use such a story so that people may understand. "Mother" had an almost absolutely positive image in Japan. The negative aspect of the Mother came rather suddenly to people's attention after receiving influences from Western culture and recognizing the merit of the "modern" ego. Young people had to begin fighting against the smothering mother, for instance. This promoted the development of Japanese consciousness.

Several years after I had begun practicing analysis, I suddenly noticed that over one-third of my analysands were Christian. (Only one percent of the population was Christian.) I thought this situation was not accidental. Japanese who are attracted to the Western ego and who also have a religious orientation often are interested in Christianity. I have such a tendency myself. When I was young, I never looked at a Buddhist *sutra*, but I remember that I read the Bible and was deeply moved. The interest of so many of my analysands in Christianity indicated that, within their Japanese culture, they had experienced some sort of friction with their surroundings and no longer felt at ease with themselves. Thus they came for analysis.

When their dream analyses began, however, they were surprised that they had highly significant dreams of Shinto shrines and Buddhist temples. Of course I never encouraged them to quit being Christian or to become Buddhist. Although this did happen in some cases during the process of dream analysis, I was devoted simply to following each one's individuation process. Concerning Buddhist connections, I had the following experience with a client. He was a nineteen-year-old young man who had a strong fear of blushing

in front of people, and this made him entirely housebound.
After several years of analysis, his symptom subsided. As we
were preparing for the termination of his therapy, he had
this dream:

> In the garden by my window is a statue of a reclining
> Bodhisattva.
> I'm peeking into the house through the window talking
> to my mother and brother inside. Now, all by myself, I must
> go out from my house into the world where there is no one I
> can trust. I'm scared, but this is the adventure I've got to do.
> At this moment, the Bodhisattva glances about and then
> he gets up. He is alive! I am relieved to see that he actually is
> alive, because I had been suspicious of the statue from the
> time I had discovered it. In the world outside of my house,
> Japanese language is not used. Since I can speak a little Ko-
> rean, I think I will manage somehow. And, without a word
> being spoken, I understand that the Bodhisattva is going to
> come along with me. My mother and brother encourage me
> to go with him. Since I'm terribly insecure going by myself, I
> have to take the chance, trust as much as possible, and go
> with him. Before we start, the Bodhisattva teaches me Korean
> pronunciation. It is quite interesting, and so now we are ready
> to go.

This dream was a turning point enabling this client to
decide clearly on terminating therapy. It seemed that if the
Bodhisattva went along with him, then he would feel safe.
He did not need to depend on his analyst any longer. I was
moved by the way this man, who had such a strong fear of
going out, acquired an inner "companion" and thus could end
the therapeutic relationship. Especially since neither the client nor I was at all interested in Buddhism, we were surprised
to see the Bodhisattva appear so prominently in his dream.
Yet, even after this profound experience, I did not have any
desire to approach Buddhism, so deep-seated was my resistance to it.

7. No Cure, Please

When introducing Jungian psychotherapy in Japan, I was afraid that, if I were to talk about dream analysis carelessly, I would be branded "unscientific." So I decided first to introduce sandplay therapy to the general public. Since we already had the tradition of *bonkei* [tray scenes] and *hako niwa* [small sandbox gardens], this nonverbal visual communication seemed rather comfortable. Showing slides of sandplay works made the direct function of images easily understandable to an audience. Although I was also doing dream analysis, I decided to encourage other clinicians to start with sandplay therapy. This approach was successful, as sandplay therapy spread all over Japan.

At first I did not teach about the symbolism which appeared in the sandtrays, nor did I make any mention of mandalas. I stressed the quality of the relationship between therapist and client as the first priority. The importance of allowing clients to express themselves freely also was emphasized as crucial for effective therapy.

After I had received reports, one after another, of successful sandplay therapy, I began to be asked to comment on these cases. Through such opportunities, I started to explain symbolism. The most interesting things occurred in regard to mandalas. Therapists noticed that, even if neither client nor therapist had previously known about these emblems, a mandala bearing important meaning often appeared at the most critical moment. From then on, I talked about the mandala, as I believed therapists and others, through their own experiences, could grasp its meaning.

In order to explain these things, I researched the mandala in Tantric Buddhism and also listened to commentary by specialists. After this research, my key concern was that I could become too involved in the complex academic study of Buddhist symbols and easily lose sight of the whole person sitting before me.

With those people who already had grasped the significance of symbols and images through sandplay therapy, I started to discuss the meanings of dreams. This teaching then was received with almost no resistance. As I have stressed, it took considerable time to come to this point. I already had waited patiently until it was the correct time to talk about fairy tales and myth.

In doing psychotherapy, I have utilized dream analysis, painting, sandplay, and sometimes only conversation—each according to my clients' needs. When the ego is so weak that the client will be easily affected by unconscious activity or easily become merely a naive "believer in dreams," it is preferable to have only conversation.

Although I felt my therapy becoming increasingly successful, much of what I knew I learned from my clients. This was essential since, being the one Jungian analyst in Japan, I did not have persons with whom I could consult. Here is one example of how I learned from a client.

I was working for a while with a middle-aged woman. But I had a hard time with her; her symptom would not change. I did not suggest sandplay for her, because I thought she would resist "just playing." But one day I pushed myself to see if she would respond. She began to work at the sandtray with much more involvement than I had expected. I did not say anything about her tray at that time. However, seeing how and what she did, I felt: "Great! Now I can cure her!"

At the next session I invited her to do sandplay. She refused, to my amazement. "Why?" I asked.

"I don't want to be cured," she said. "I'm not coming here to be cured."

"Then why are you here?" I asked.

"I come here just to come here."

This statement taught me a lot. Now I realize that I can't "cure" people. I have already mentioned that you cannot apply the "theory" of Depth Psychology to the client. But we are fully accustomed to thinking in terms of modern technology: if it's broken, you fix it. We tend to fall into thinking in a manipulative way, an operational mode. "Cure by sandplay therapy" is the most blatant example of such thinking. The patient was accurately picking up on such an attitude and re-fused the "cure." Yet, as I continued to sit with her, without focusing on curing her, her symptoms disappeared.

The most important thing in psychotherapy is that two people are there for each other. These two shouldn't be differ-entiated as "healer" and "healed one." I should say that, while two people are "being" together, a phenomenon called "cure" frequently happens as a by-product. This, of course, made me consider seriously what the therapist is doing. What is the therapist's role? This then eventually led me to realize that Buddhism had great meaning to me. I was not following Bud-dhist ideas in order to do psychotherapy. Rather, I began to notice, as I reflected upon the meaning of my psychotherapy, that the teachings of Buddhism had become useful.

8. Finding a Teacher in Japan

The Buddhist monk, Myoe (1173–1232), recorded his dreams throughout his life. This record has been preserved as his dream diary. For many years friends had suggested that I study this diary, but because of my negative feelings toward Bud-dhism, I never was quite willing to work on it. But when once I happened upon it, I began reading that diary of dreams and was most impressed. I thought that this person was a rare be-ing indeed!

As I have mentioned, all of the teachers to whom I looked up, in terms of my individuation process, were West-erners. Unfortunately, I never met C. G. Jung; but the strong-est support for my heart always came from him. As a Japanese, I regretted not being able to find a Japanese teacher as well. But when I read Myoe's dream diary, I felt that finally I had been able to find one. Then I devoured biographies of Myoe and essays about him, one after another. My feeling of having found my teacher did not waver but grew deeper and deeper.

Guided by Myoe, I started to read Buddhist sutras, and I felt I was growing closer to Buddhism. The more I understood Buddhism, the more I found that my psychotherapy was deeply related to what Buddhist sutras deal with. I read the *Avatamsaka [Garland] Sutra*, or *Kegon Kyo* in Japanese, which was the primary sutra for the Kegon sect, to which Myoe belonged. One of the effects of reading it is the tendency to fall asleep after awhile. For instance, at the beginning, the Universal Buddha, Vairocana, appears, and the many gods surrounding him praise and praise him. Then twenty great Bodhisattvas' entire formal names are all stated. In addition, the ten great guardians surrounding them are all fully introduced. Then other gods' names follow them and on and on and on . . . perhaps almost two hundred elaborate names, though I've never counted them. As you read those names one by one, they all sound rather similar.

Eventually one of them praises the Buddha, and the praises continue on and on. When reading it rather absentmindedly, I felt like saying, "So, what is the nub of all of this?" But I just bore with it, and while I kept reading that most blessed message, I fell asleep.

I was at a loss. I wondered how Myoe, whom I looked up to, had responded to this sutra. Then I realized that probably he had not read this sutra. Monks did not "read," they chanted it. It was in chanting the sutra, while repeating many similar and gracious names, that transformation of consciousness was to be expected.

You can approach the sutra only through this sort of consciousness. It seems that it is in this manner that its true "content" can become "comprehensible," content which seems close to saying simply, "Light. Light. Light. All shines, all filled with Light." Elusive and almost ineffable, something is yet most certainly transmitted through this chanting. If you ask what that is, it is nearly impossible to answer. It seems that it has no name.

After all, the Vairocana Buddha situated in the center of all this, surprisingly enough, says nothing, not even one word. The *Avatamsaka* is a voluminous sutra, but not one word is uttered anywhere in it by this Buddha Vairocana. One among

the Bodhisattvas surrounding the great Buddha narrates, receiving divine energy. During this time, Vairocana Himself,
rather than speaking, emits light from between his teeth.

Not able to chant this sutra by myself I read it as if chanting, then dozed, chanted, dozed . . . While doing this, I felt
that psychotherapy is basically quite similar. Jung took
dreams seriously. This means that he gave weight to the reality which is grasped by extra-ordinary consciousness, which
is truly different from the ordinary. In Jung, you reach the
dream world starting from the modern ego; in Kegon, you
seem to be right in the middle of the dream world from the
beginning.

The modern Western ego was developed by making ordinary consciousness autonomous and refined. As it gained the
weapon of so-called natural science, it seemed that its power
might overwhelm the whole world. In contrast, consciousness as defined by Buddhism developed in the opposite direction. There is no concept of efficiency or manipulation at
all. What there is seems to be useless for anything, yet it has
the capacity to heal the illness from which the modern ego
suffers.

Not being Vairocana Buddha, light does not shine out
between my teeth, but I am becoming more silent. Before,
when listening to dreams, I understood them, so I "interpreted" them. But now I'm less and less inclined to interpret.
Dreams are important, so I listen, and more often now I
only listen.

Guided by Teacher Myoe, attracted to the world of
Kegon, I think my attitude toward analysis has changed
somewhat. I don't mean that I have switched from Jung to
Myoe, for I believe both are my teachers. Some could say,
however, that it's strange, since the term *Jungian* means one
who looks up only to Jung as her or his teacher.

For such people, just listening to dreams and not strain-
ing after archetypes, not making interpretations but just
being there in what might appear to be an absentminded
fashion, certainly is not Jungian. According to such thinking,

I would not be a Jungian. But then, according to those who live by strict definitions, I may not be a Buddhist either.

But I myself feel that I am a Jungian. Why so? What does that word *Jungian* mean?

9. What Is a Jungian?

To me, to be a Jungian means to observe conscientiously and attentively the material produced by the unconscious and then to live one's life upon that foundation, going forward with one's own individuation process. For this purpose, one should master the basic knowledge and skills required. Obviously there are going to be many individual differences among Jungians, depending upon how a person has dealt with materials from the unconscious. If one finds that his way of individuation differs from what C. G. Jung has worked out, then one should make a great effort to clarify why and how it is so. It is important not to ignore the simplicity of the point that the individuation process leads to individual differences which are expected.

Given what I have described, I seem to be a Jungian. Of course, if there is a person who thinks that being a Jungian means following completely what C. G. Jung said, taking that as entirely correct, then surely I am not a Jungian. On the other hand, if a Jungian is simply one who follows her or his own individuation process, then one is a Jungian no matter what one does, as long as one stays on track. But this seems a bit too easy, too simplistic. I would say that you are a Jungian when, in order to avoid your own arbitrariness or self-indulgent living, you choose C. G. Jung as a reference point for your self-examination, in which you challenge completely your beliefs and methods and find positive meaning in doing that. When you stop finding meaning in that, then I think you would stop being a Jungian. "Jungian" means, not following Jung completely, but finding the positive meaning in confronting Jung and in rigorously comparing his approach with yours.

Even though I am a Jungian, you would understand that,

when I as an Asian try to identify what I have experienced, the result is not the same as what Jung has done. My way of consciousness differs from the European, and also my relation to the unconscious is different.

If we emphasize the individuation aspect of the process, it seems reasonable just to choose your own way of developing, without calling it Jungian or Freudian. But the interesting part is your personality. It is actually positively meaningful to choose a school of thought. That is because, without a framework within which to develop your individuality, you easily get lost or fall into arbitrariness. By choosing a certain school, you can commit yourself. Then you have a framework or frame of reference for checking your own way of life.

On the other hand, if you depend entirely upon your connection to a certain school, your individuation process will be hindered. Sometimes the founder of the school becomes a guru, and the theory becomes a dogma. The choice of schools has this double aspect which we all need to remember.

So what about Buddhism? I think Buddhism is a highly tolerant religion. As it migrated to Japan, the degree of its tolerance increased. Therefore, there does not seem to be any problem in saying that I am both a Jungian and a Buddhist. Of course, even in Buddhism, strictly speaking, you need to choose a sect. Then, however, there is a certain doctrine, ritual, and means for the maintenance of the sect, and this causes me to defer becoming a temple member. I sometimes feel that this may counteract or become detrimental in terms of the individuation process. Groups as such, particularly in Japan, tend to work against the modern Western ego (the individual). One needs to be cautious about belonging to a particular group. I do oppose the idea that the way of the modern Western ego is the only way for us, though I recognize fully its positive aspect. I wish to function in the Western way or the Japanese way according to the situation. I said that I look up to Myoe as my spiritual teacher, but Myoe himself was not interested in founding a sect. He struggled to avoid religious sects and orders at that time. So, even though I say that I respect Myoe as a teacher, I don't mean to belong to his sect. Truly to follow his way, I must go alone. Thus, he does not allow me to become his "disciple" easily.

When I carry on this sort of argument, I have to keep repeating the phrase "cannot say I am this or that definitely." Maybe I should say that I am a "vague" Buddhist. I do have a great deal of confidence in being vague [*aimai*]. This confidence is supported by my thirty-year experience of analytical practice, during which I feel I was trained largely by many of my clients. Based on this "vague" standpoint of mine, I will continue this discussion of my experiences related to Buddhism.

Chapter 2

◢◤◥◣◢◤◥◣◢◤◥◣◢◤◥◣◢◤◥◣

The "Ten Oxherding Pictures" and Alchemy

◢◤◥◣◢◤◥◣◢◤◥◣◢◤◥◣◢◤◥◣

The first time I saw the "Ten Oxherding Pictures" was in the United States of America. It is embarrassing to admit, as I did in the first chapter, that I did not even know that such paintings existed in the East. I was deeply moved when Dr. Spiegelman showed me the version of the series painted by the fifteenth-century Japanese painter Shubun, based on the ideas of Kuo-an.[1]

I have mentioned that I had some affinity with Zen Buddhism, although at that time I was rejecting nearly everything Japanese. I was attracted to the experience of sudden enlightenment in Zen. I had two responses to it: (1) How wonderful it would be to have such an experience! and (2) I had no way to attain such an experience. It seemed self-evident that, no matter how much effort I might expend, it would not be possible for me to have instant enlightenment.

Despite this attitude, seeing those ten pictures was quite exciting to me, because the change was shown in ten stages. Right away I read the commentary by D. T. Suzuki[2] and found that my view was shallow, because the change did not take place in as developmental a manner as I initially had assumed. A different set of pictures by Pu-ming[3] displayed a much fresher, more progressive quality compared with Kuo-an's, which illustrated the "instant enlightenment" [*tongo*] point of view.

My interest in these pictures continued. I read many commentaries, and later, when I started to teach at Kyoto University, my colleague, Professor Shizuteru Ueda, an expert on the Zen "Oxherding" genre, gave me many useful insights.[4] Then, in 1982, Dr. Spiegelman and Dr. Mokusen Miyuki, a Japanese Jungian analyst residing in Los Angeles, came to Japan, where we held a symposium together on these same pictures. Very recently, after more than ten years had passed and I needed to begin preparing for these lectures, I again planned a symposium on the "Ten Oxherding Pictures." This time, Dr. Miyuki and I were joined by a well-known scholar of Buddhism, Dr. Yuichi Kajiyama. These two symposia taught me a great deal, and I will refer to material from them. I must, however, make it quite clear that, in saying what I do, I am not speaking as a "scholar" of these paintings or of Buddhism. Instead, this is only my own impression as a layman whose specialty is psychotherapy.

1. The "Oxherding Pictures"

Since some of you readers may be quite familiar with these pictures, I shall sketch only a brief background. This traditional series of pictures illustrating development in Zen practice is called "Ten Oxherding Pictures" or simply the "Oxherding Pictures," as there are not necessarily ten. Although their origin is unknown, they became widely distributed in China and Japan, and various kinds exist at the present time. Pu-ming's paintings, for example, describe a process indicated through the gradual whitening of a black ox, while Kuo-an's follow a "sudden enlightenment" view, without such a process. According to Dr. Kajiyama, Tibetans use elephant-herding pictures instead, but the elephant also gradually becomes white.[5]

Let's look at the paintings which express Kuo-an's view. I will discuss simply how I, as an amateur, see them, leaving the elucidation of the Buddhist view to Dr. D. T. Suzuki. The

Fig. 1. Searching for the Ox

Fig. 2. Seeing the Traces

Fig. 3. Seeing the Ox

Fig. 4. Catching the Ox

Fig. 5. Herding the Ox

Fig. 6. Coming Home on the Ox's Back

*Fig. 7. The Ox Forgotten,
Leaving the Man Alone*

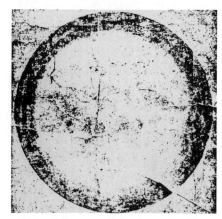
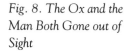

*Fig. 8. The Ox and the
Man Both Gone out of
Sight*

*Fig. 9. Returning to the
Origin, Back to the Source*

Fig. 10. Entering the City with Bliss-bestowing Hands.

first picture, "Searching for the Ox," shows a young man looking for something in the meadow. Next comes "Seeing Traces." No. 3 is "Seeing the Ox"; No. 4 is "Catching the Ox"; and No. 5 is "Herding the Ox." Viewing these pictures together, it becomes clear to anyone that the young man, who was alone at the beginning, finds the ox and then gradually tames it.

But eventually we all wonder, "What is the ox?" According to the Zen school, the ox is "self" or "true self." But when I ponder this matter further, I realize that, for me, the ox could not be the true self. I could say that, for the youth, his relationship to the Self at that moment creates such an image. In this view, the Self exists even in the first picture. But the youth, somehow, although he doesn't know why, feels that there is something he needs to search for, but it seems completely vague, like something without form. Then to him this condition manifests as the ox, a "presence" which he begins to relate to. Then he "catches" it and "herds" it. Eventually he finds that he does not need to manage it any longer. So, in No. 6 we have him "Coming Home on the Ox's Back," and he is playing music, letting the ox choose the way. This attitude differs greatly from that evident in No. 5, in which the youth was guiding the ox.

It is most interesting, as Ueda and Yanagita comment,[6] that the process from No. 1 through No. 6 is always reversible. That is to say, the youth playing the flute in No. 6 might think that the ox is going in the wrong direction, so then he might feel that he should lead the ox. Then the ox suddenly might become excited and get wild. From there we might end up at No. 1, reversing the progress. No matter how far you have advanced, don't forget the possibility of slipping back.

Viewing these six in a Jungian perspective, with the youth and the ox indicating the relationship between ego and Self, the sixth may well be said to represent the pinnacle. Here the ego completely relinquishes its initiative to the Self, by which it is being led. The ego sings its own feelings, and the world surrounding it is also peaceful. But this series indicates a further process. What a surprise to find that, in No. 7, "Ox Forgotten," the ox disappears! Indeed, man and the ox have become completely one.

This sort of understanding is generally accepted, but I think that the Self now is manifested not as an ox but as the external environment surrounding the person, taken as a whole. In No. 1, the person was there all alone. In that sense, No. 7 is the same. However, in No. 1, the person was there with some sort of feeling of loss. In No. 7, you might be able to see everything surrounding the person as her or his "Self," in a Jungian sense. It is interesting that Kuo-an's inscription for his second painting states: "Embodying all things as self." Then he continues, "He [the youth] has no discrimination between good and evil or true and false. That is to say, he embodies everything as self." No. 7 at first may appear to be quite undifferentiated in terms of self-image and a sense of reality. However, one might say that here it is a conscious undifferentiation, rather than the unconscious undifferentiation of No. 1. It may be an awareness of no separateness or no independent nature.

It is quite interesting to contrast Nos. 1 and 7. In appearance, they are similar. Therefore a person in the state depicted in No. 7 might be assessed as having no capacity to discriminate or as being absentminded, as though at the level of picture 1. And if a person thinks himself to be in the state of No. 7, he suddenly may start to see traces of the ox here and there or feel that, attacked by feelings of loss, he cannot grasp his true situation. So once again he wishes to catch the ox.

What I like about this series of pictures is that, one by one, they provoke our imagination. In my case, they make me think over my own situation as well as my client's. Between Nos. 6 and 7 is a jump, but between No. 7 and No. 8 there is a real leap. I still remember the impact of this transition when I saw the series for the first time. Somehow I could expect the ox to disappear, but is it all right for the person also to disappear? Then, who is this looking at the circle? This was my honest feeling at that time. Now, looking at this, I am able to suppose the existence of such a state. But, since I have never experienced it, I cannot affirm it wholeheartedly. This is, simply speaking, the *experience* of death, of Absolute Nothingness. In this school of practice, there is no higher state that one could wish to attain. The tenth picture by Pu-ming shows such a state, reflecting this point. We should consider that the two pictures by Kuo-an which follow No. 8 quite possibly are not meant to be developmentally higher. Ueda and Yanagita explain that 8, 9, and 10 are not positioned as steps of development: "The relationship of mutual penetration is immediately reversible."[7]

Picture No. 9, "Return to the Source," is a painting of a flowing river and a blossoming tree. Ueda sees the transition from No. 8 to No. 9 as "after the cessation, again reviving." At this point, Zen people get into deep and difficult theory, but to me it seems more interesting to think that, since the following picture shows human beings revived from death, human beings would be experiencing "mineral consciousness" and "vegetative consciousness" at this point. These states need not be called "consciousness." But, if you can deal with "Absolute Nothingness" (No. 8), it certainly must be possible to experience animal and vegetative consciousnesses of some sort. Of course, this is just my own arbitrary assumption.

Two human beings are presented in the tenth picture, "Entering the City with Bliss-bestowing Hands." Ueda explains that "this last painting never indicates that the old person, who represents the self, having passed through various stages, is meeting the young person by accident. The True Self is becoming two who are facing each other."[8] Two people are united as one body. However, this union is not similar to the union of the two human beings in the tenth picture of the *Rosarium Philosophorum*, which we will soon discuss.

It is interesting that here, even though there is a space between them, these two people are one. This means that there is the possibility of the emergence of dialogue between them: "Who are you?" "Where are you from?" and so on. And there is the possibility of leading back to the first picture. The tenth picture seems to show completion, but it also indicates a return to the beginning.

I have discussed now how I see this picture series. Next I would like to say how I as a psychotherapist felt about these "Oxherding Pictures."

2. Instant Enlightenment and Insight

The pictures by Pu-ming present the black ox gradually transforming into a white one; during this process, it is necessary for the ox to be tamed. There are great differences between this version and Kuo-an's. Pu-ming's pictures are drawn in a square and end with the emergence of the circle as the tenth picture, whereas all of Kuo-an's are drawn in a circle from the beginning. As to the process of enlightenment, these two series reflect the difference of opinion between "instant enlightenment" (*tongo*, Kuo-an) and "gradual enlightenment" (*zango*, Pu-ming] viewpoints.

Leaving these theoretical disputes to specialists, what will happen if we look at these pictures in relation to our psychotherapeutic situation? Kuo-an's first picture indicates the situation: not able to see even the ox's traces, completely lost.

The picture is, however, surrounded by a circle, and the inscription on it reads: "From the beginning, never lost; why search?" This corresponds to our therapeutic stance: when we meet a client who is lost, unable to find any sign of resolution, we are still able to see the person without losing hope. Even if we meet a person who thinks that he or she has lost everything and that the situation is in no way recoverable, it is important for us to have the "never lost" attitude. You don't need desperately to think how to get it back—all in a great rush.

We must realize, of course, that the thing which the client wants to regain "because it's lost" and the thing about which we think "it's not lost" may be different. But if you know that, in the end, the most important issue is the circle or the containment of the therapeutic relationship, then I think you will be well centered.

One day a certain older woman came, complaining about how much she was suffering because of her daughter-in-law, who had "such an ill character." At that time it was still usual in Japan for the oldest son's family to live with the son's mother. According to this moral standard, then, the daughter-in-law should have been serving the mother. Interestingly enough, this mother was the one who had selected this daughter-in-law as the best wife for her son. Then he had just gone along with his mother's choice. When they were actually living all together, the daughter-in-law's demerits alone stood out. In this case, if the mother were right, then her daughter-in-law would have been an absolutely terrible woman. What to do now in this situation was the mother's problem. She had come to consult me, asking, "What shall I do?"

Suddenly I remembered an old Buddhist story familiar to older people, "Ushini hikarete, Zenkoji mairi" ["Drawn by a Cow, Worshipping at Zenkoji"]. This is the story of an old woman who was greedy and had no faith. One day she had hung out a fine cloth to dry. The neighbor's cow happened to snag it on her horns, so the woman chased after it, running on and on. Without realizing it, she ran into Zenkoji Temple. When she realized it was a holy place, she prayed for her afterlife. This is the story of an act committed out of greed that, without realizing it, turned out to awaken faith.

My client knew the story, so I said to her, "Your daughter-in-law is the Zenkoji cow." She was perplexed. I added, "Getting angry at your daughter-in-law, running after her, you end up going to Zenkoji." She did not seem to get it, but continued to come for sessions. She kept talking about how terrible her daughter-in-law was. "What shall I do? Is there any good remedy for this?" she lamented. My reply to her was always the same: "There is no remedy for this."

Her later recollection of this scenario was: "There was no real answer, so every session I thought, 'We need to stop.' But then I remembered, 'Worshipping at Zenkoji.' And I decided to continue anyway." While we kept on going, she was being guided by her dreams. Deepening her interest in the religious world, she prepared for aging and death. The client despaired many times, but the circle surrounding us was never destroyed. Although she started to come to these sessions in order to do something about her daughter-in-law, the search for the Self had begun at that moment. I communicated that idea to her somehow, in using the Buddhist story.

This client, enduring much suffering, felt like quitting many times over a long period. Then gradually she entered into the religious realm. Some people therefore might see this as gradual enlightenment. But I think the key point of the philosophy of sudden enlightenment is the possibility that "enlightenment" exists from the beginning, although the process involved in reaching it may be gradual.

Contrary to this, following the idea of gradual enlightenment, maintaining the daily practice, it may happen that suddenly you get enlightened. There may not be too much difference between the two ways. Being mistaken about "sudden *satori* [enlightenment]" and omitting necessary effort, or being possessed by gradual satori and becoming overly involved in unnecessarily heavy practice—either can be a problem.

Despite having no experience of enlightenment, I give my amateur opinion regarding the issue of *satori* because I approach it as related to "insight" in psychotherapy. When I began psychotherapy, I was captured by the thought that I would encounter a suffering client who instantly would be released from the problematical situation after having a wonderful experience of "insight." And it would have been the "interpretation" that I had offered which was most helpful in achieving such a change.

But actually, of course, I am incapable of "giving" anything. The client walks her or his own path of individuation. So-called "insight" may help, but the client rarely reaches full resolution through it. Even though one has insight, the process advances gradually. And, as I mentioned in comments on the "Oxherding Pictures," the process could reverse—even after having insight. Going back and forth, I believe the therapist has to maintain a strong trust in the circle which encloses the whole, and just continue being there. Otherwise, the therapist may force unnecessarily hard practice, telling the client to do this, do that, etc., based on a mistaken "gradual enlightenment" approach.

3. Rosarium Philosophorum

The *Rosarium* pictures of alchemy in "The Psychology of Transference," by C. G. Jung, reminded me of the "Oxherding Pictures."[9]

The *Rosarium* pictures were originally for alchemy. Jung noticed that the process of transformation in metals described in it could be interpreted as symbolic expression of the process of personality change. He tried to find in this series of pictures a process of transformation which would occur in the psyche of therapist and patient. The main theme of the series is "conjunction." A king and a queen take off their clothes and submerge themselves in water, to be united. Then they have to die, and their conjoined soul ascends to heaven. After purification, the soul returns. In the end a new birth comes, with a real unity of male and female. This kind of

Fig. 11. The Mercurial
Fountain

Fig. 12. King and Queen

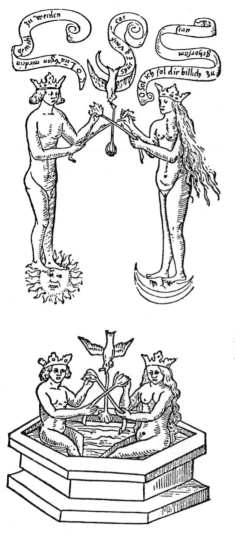

Fig. 13. The Naked Truth

*Fig. 14. Immersion in the
Bath*

Fig. 15. The Conjunction

Fig. 16. Death

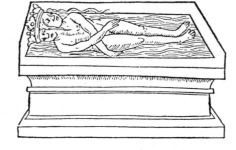

Fig. 17. The Ascent of the Soul

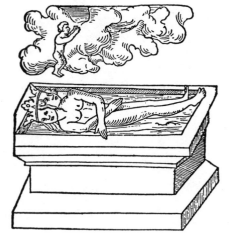

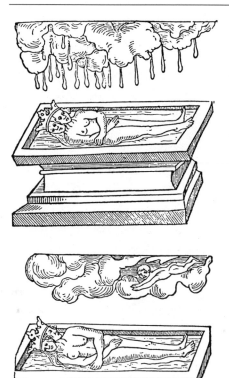

Fig. 18. Purification

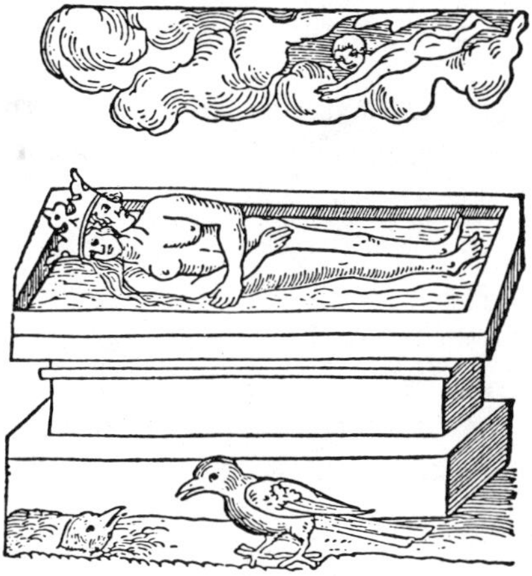

Fig. 19. The Return of the Soul

Fig. 20. The New Birth

"conjunction" symbolizes, according to Jung, the process of individuation, which therapist and patient both experience in the course of therapy.

Both series have ten pictures illustrating the individuation process, but there are great differences between them. Since I am always comparing East and West, I could not resist comparing these two different sets of pictures. Dr. Marvin Spiegelman also discussed the *Rosarium Philosophorum* in his commentary on the "Oxherding Pictures,"[10] and I am in general agreement with his views.

Here I would like to compare these two series which are so very different. But first we might try, just for fun, applying the titles of the *Rosarium* pictures to Kuo-an's series; the results appear in Table 1.

Table 1. Comparing Two Series of Pictures

Kuo-an No.	Kuo-an Title	Rosarium Title
No. 1	Searching for the Ox	The Mercurial Fountain
No. 2	Seeing Traces	King and Queen
No. 3	Seeing the Ox	The Naked Truth

No. 4	Catching the Ox	Immersion in the Bath
No. 5	Herding the Ox	The Conjunction
No. 6	Coming Home on the Ox's Back	Death
No. 7	The Ox Forgotten	The Ascent of the Soul
No. 8	The Man and the Ox Both Forgotten	Purification
No. 9	Return to the Origin, Back to the Source	The Return of the Soul
No. 10	Entering the City with Bliss-bestowing Hands	The New Birth

Since these titles were given to completely different series, the close correspondence is quite surprising. Even the sixth, "Death," and the eighth, "Purification," are closely related. The sixth "Oxherding Picture" corresponds to death in the sense that, when led by nature, you return to the earth. I spoke of the eighth as "revival after death." At such a moment, you can naturally imagine that there would be an experience of "purification."

Considering all this, I was rather deeply struck by the similarity of the two sets of pictures, created as separate series and coming from completely different cultures. This mysterious similarity exists, I think, because both sets are trying to express the search for the Self, which Jung was so involved in describing.

I think you cannot illustrate the Self itself. It is only possible to express it through the image of the Self which one can make conscious at any given moment. Consequently, if different people try to illustrate any process of searching for the Self, the results will show considerable differences, due to the variety of ways in which consciousness grasps it. Comparing these series means, then, comparing in general the ways of consciousness of East and West.

It is not clear what sort of consciousness created the *Rosarium Philosophorum*—whether the desire was to write the process of chemical change or to illustrate the process of the transformation of personality. Probably the effort consciously included both aspects as one. In contrast, the "Oxherding Pictures" consciously were intended to describe stages approaching enlightenment in Zen practice.

Since Jung views the *Rosarium Philosophorum* series as a depiction of the transference process given in the alchemical mode, his ego is outside these pictures. From this outside position, he analyzes and interprets them as an "unconscious process." In contrast, in the "Oxherding Pictures," the ego as the young man is that of the maker of the series (and of the viewer as well). It/he is included within the picture. This is a major difference. The one who interprets is in the phenomenon.

It must be further recognized that, in the case of the "Oxherding Pictures," the "ego" in this pairing is not the same as the "ego" of Western discourse. The Western ego defines itself clearly and objectifies the "unconscious process" as illustrated, though in actuality it may not be this clear. In the "Oxherding Pictures," the consciousness of the maker/viewer is depicted, and it has the nature or tendency even to disappear in mid-process. In order to consider such a phenomenon closely, in place of the concept of "ego" I think it is better to use "level of consciousness." I will expand upon this view in chapter 3.

The most impressive aspect of the *Rosarium*'s illustrations of alchemy was the importance accorded the image of the union of masculine and feminine. The point we need to attend to is the establishment of the conscious ego. To such an ego, it is meaningful to have the image of the union of masculine and feminine take place in the unconscious process. If it is simply the union of male and female, then it is indeed an ordinary matter, because nonhuman animal species also are capable of that. It is important to think about the meaning of sequence. The "Conjunction" of the *Rosarium* comes in the

fifth place, not the tenth. After that comes death. In the Eastern series, the attitude of the youth is transformed from
working hard to catch the ox to forgetting the ox. This fifth-
picture movement seems to parallel that of the *Rosarium's*
fifth picture. And the last stage in the *Rosarium* is illustrated
not as "Conjunction," but as "New Birth."

Keeping the image of masculine and feminine in the
Western series in mind, then, we cannot help noticing, when
looking at the "Oxherding" series, that there is no feminine
figure in it. This is important. I loved to read fairy tales from
a very young age. But I didn't understand why, when there
were lots of stories—in Grimm's tales, for instance—with
happy endings in marriage, very few cases like those existed
in Japanese tales. Japanese stories often end in what appears
to be a situation of no change, and sometimes they end in
tragedy. In the Japanese works, the hero, at the end, often is
left in the same position he occupied in the beginning. His
experience, however, has brought him to the point of conscious undifferentiation, as in the movement from No. 1 to
No. 7 of the "Oxherding Pictures."

4. Anima Figure

Jung thought that the image of a male's soul appears as a feminine figure (*anima*). After seeing many male analysands, he
found that there were characteristic feminine figures who appeared in their dreams. He also researched ancient Western
mythology and fairy tales deeply. After all this analytical and
scholarly inquiry, he arrived at this conclusion.

In my own way, as I have accumulated analytical experience in Japan, I too have seen that characteristic feminine
figures appear in Japanese men's dreams. I also have realized
that it is meaningful to interpret these as soul images. But the
four developmental stages of the anima, well known in Jungian circles, do not occur similarly in many cases. Also, in
some cases the feminine figure in dreams is not very important. Therefore, instead of thinking that Japanese people
are at immature stages in the individuation process, I started

to see that the process takes different forms of expression. For instance, you may see the ox in the pictures as the soul image.

In the West, the anima figure was mostly represented by a female figure. I think this is related to the fact that the Western ego was represented by the male hero figure. Neumann, unlike Freudians, who would interpret it as killing the Father, thought that the hero's dragon fight was a symbolic expression of killing the Mother.[11] After he accomplished that killing—i.e., the cutting of his containment in the unconscious uroboric Mother—the now independent hero again tries to establish a relationship to the feminine in the depths of the unconscious. That was when the hero's union with the feminine appeared. This symbolism is highly significant. Such a plot seems clear and reasonable, and the meaning of the feminine is obvious here.

Here is a dream reported by a Japanese psychotherapist.[12] He was my student when he was in graduate school. While he had an adolescent female client who was suffering from school refusal as well as dermatitis, her father also started therapy with him. Three generations of this family were living together. The therapist felt that the father was too weak, not taking a stand in the appropriate "father's role"; this weakness he thought was the problem of the multigenerational family. The therapist was frustrated by this father, who was far from being the "strong father" he felt the man should be, even though he was getting better. At that time, the therapist had this dream:

> The dreamer caught two green snakes at a construction site. He realized that these gigantic snakes with four legs were the father's pets. While the father was showing one of them to the dreamer, the other snake was staring at the dreamer, and there was tension, as if it might jump quickly at any minute. The father, controlling the one, maneuvered the other one with a stick into the box where they had come from, so it would not attack the dreamer.

After this dream, the therapist's view of the father changed. He had thought of him as being an inadequate father and wanted him to take the role of a "strong" father who would kill snakes like this. But this dream indicated that this "weak" father was a strong person who could handle gigantic snakes. The father in the dream did not simply kill the one threatening serpent; instead, he was capable of handling both serpents skillfully. In the dream, the father "appeared to have the aura of a craftsman: confident, steady, and calm. He saved me with his concentration and judgment from moment to moment." The therapist further commented, "I was arrogantly thinking of him as inadequate, but, contrary to that, I started to think that even I may have been helped by his wisdom."

I was very impressed with this case. This therapist, who was my student, thought, perhaps because of my influence, that a father should be strong—strong enough to kill a snake; and he was trying to do therapy along that line. Through his own dream, he started to think that it might be good to have a father who had the wisdom to manage a snake. So the therapist, who had been trying to guide the father according to the strong-father thesis, now, to the contrary, realized that he could be guided by this father's wisdom.

Now, I wonder, would the image of the soul of this father be represented by a feminine figure? It seems quite suitable, if not natural, to think that the two gigantic green serpents are his soul image. Or should these great snakes, as in the German Romantic writer E. T. A. Hoffmann's novel,[13] transform themselves into women? Recently I have been thinking that, if they stayed as serpents, fine; if they changed into women, fine. Each way has its own meaning. You cannot judge one as better than the other.

It must be the result of Christian influence that the anima figure is represented by a female. Jung described Christianity as a religion in which the masculine principle is dominant. To compensate, femininity gradually was recognized, even in Christian culture. One of the early means was al-

chemy. Therefore the union of masculine and feminine in alchemy has a profound symbolic meaning; the feminine figure,
as the anima image, was valued highly.

Now let us consider the feminine in Buddhism. In the
early days of Buddhism, when the Buddha preached, it seems
that women were rather outside of consideration. Initially all
the ordained followers were men. Once ordained, they re-
mained single throughout their lives. In Buddhism it is important to keep the precepts. One of the first rules was having
no sexual intercourse with women. After men were ordained
and learning how to attain Nirvana, it was necessary to aban-
don all attachments, beginning with attachment to women.
Such rules must have been established because of the considerable difficulty in relinquishing attachments. However, even
if Buddhism was taught especially for men, it does not mean
that Buddhism is based on a masculine principle. I will discuss
the way of consciousness in Buddhism in detail below, as it
differs greatly from the Western masculine principle.

When Mahayana Buddhism gained strength in East Asia,
it became clearer that Buddhist redemption was based on the
maternal principle. Therefore, although Buddhism seemed
close to rejecting women, it was paradoxically relying on the
maternal principle, because everyone was equal and equally
redeemed. However, in the social structure, men were superior to women. In order to resolve this contradiction, some
early included the idea that women also are redeemable.
Thus, as Buddhism was transmitted through China and eventually to Japan, it became a religion in which the maternal
principle was dominant.

In the "Oxherding Pictures" of Kuo-an, we see no female
figure, but from the beginning to the end, there is a circle as
the unchanging framework. This seems to me to indicate the
maternal, containment. Within such unchanging, impersonal motherly protection, the drama of the ox and the youth
proceeds. Finally it takes the form of *senex* (old man) and *puer*
(youth) mutually coexisting. While there is no appearance of
a woman as an anima figure, the feminine is not ignored.

In Buddhism, the maternal nature always has been highly valued. But within that religion it certainly is difficult to find a feminine figure who resembles Western culture's romantic anima, with her relationship to a man. The "Oxherding" series indicates that difficulty. The reason I respect the Buddhist monk Myoe is that he was a rare being who had a deep relation to a feminine figure or anima. I have discussed this relationship elsewhere.[14] Even though Myoe is an exception, it made me personally very happy to discover such a monk existing in Japan in the twelfth and thirteenth centuries. Moreover, the information about him is most useful in psychological and religious thought.

5. Circle and Straight Line

An impressive sight in the "Oxherding" series is the last scene: an old man and a youth are facing each other. This youth, after departing from the old man, will return to the state in the first picture. Such a speculation comes to mind naturally. It seems to me that the tenth picture connects to the first one, and thus the series repeats itself in an infinitely circular motion. The last picture in alchemy, entitled "New Birth," also suggests that something is to come. But, much more than in the "Oxherding" series, the alchemical series seems to give the impression that the last picture is set up as a goal.

Again referring to Neumann, we students found it very helpful to see the development of ego as a symbolical progression from beginning to end in gradual steps rising in a straight line. The individuation process, as Jung presented it, proceeds from the shadow, anima, and animus archetypes to the Self archetype in such a linear sequence. The anima itself is considered to have developmental stages as well.

Although, as you know, Jung's ideas often are not clear-cut, Freud's developmental stages are fairly clear. Then there are experimental psychologists who criticize even Freud as unscientific and propose more definite developmental stages. While their work may be useful in determining if the client's development is "normal" or in indicating how "delayed" it may be, it does not help us identify what sort of psychotherapy should be applied. So, often such stage theories are not too helpful.

Now, as we have said, depth psychology begins with the "individual" and is about what happens if a certain individual starts to explore her or his own "psyche" [kokoro]. For that exploration, we would like to learn from our eminent predecessors' experiences. Then, if we focus on the surface of the human psyche, we can at least say something definite. However, as we go deeper, the psyche appears to become increasingly vague. Jung says the level of collective unconscious is filled with archetypes. Therefore it becomes nonsense to speak of developmental stages there. The child archetype, mother archetype, father archetype, etc., are all coexisting. From birth to death, all manner of archetypal beings are simultaneously coexisting. From beginning to end, there is no change.

I said that it is convenient to know about, and have illustrations of, the stages. Then you can see clients on such a scale and guide them accordingly. But it does not always work that way. I gave such an example above, one in which a therapist corrected himself after having a dream. Following Neumann's theory, he had expected too much of the "father conquers the dragon" motif. At that point, if the therapist had insisted upon Neumann's theoretical stages, the therapy probably would not have proceeded well.

Working with clients, we need to be able to look at them both with and without a theory of stages. Buddhism offers an effective way of observing without stages. The first of Kuoan's paintings is accompanied by the comment, "From the beginning, never lost; why search?" That is, "The ox never got away, so there's no need to search." Therefore, you may say that things are the same at the beginning and at the end. Thus, as the pictures are shown in a sequence from first to tenth, they appear to be indicating real stages, but that is only for convenience; it's possible to show the entire process in one painting.

Modern man likes the word *progress*. I think contemporary people are still dragging that idea around. It is easy to accept that logic which proposes a diagram of "progress," progress with stages rising in a line. On this point, Jungian ideas are pretty flexible, while Buddhism is utterly open. There is no first and last, no beginning or end. Buddhism shows us the world of everything as it is, as a whole. No real change is going on.

The *Garland Sutra* is a collection of sutras, among them the "*Juji-bon*," which illustrates the Bodhisattva process, i.e., the ten stages of becoming a Buddha. A while ago I became eager to get at some of its "developmental ideas," so I began to read it with zest. But it threw me for a loop. The first stage is called "*kanki-chi*" [joyous place]. At this stage, the Bodhisattva thinks, for example, as follows:

> *Transforming the 'self' and leaving behind the limitations*
> *of all worlds of being,*
> *the mind of Joy arises.*
> *Entering into the non-discriminating midst of all Buddhas,*
> *the mind of Joy arises.*
> *Distancing oneself from the realms of delusion,*
> *from the common world,*
> *the mind of Joy arises.*
> *Approaching the realm of Wisdom,*
> *the mind of Joy arises.*
> *Cutting oneself off from all the evil realms,*
> *the mind of Joy arises.*
> *Achieving the silencing of the mind for the sake of all sentient beings,*
> *the mind of Joy arises.*
> *Seeing closely all the Buddhas,*
> *the mind of Joy arises.*
> *Born in the realm of all Buddhas,*
> *the mind of Joy arises.*

Entering into the company of all the Bodhisattvas,
the mind of Joy arises.
Leaving behind all fears,
the mind of Joy arises.

Listening to the refrain, "kanki no kokoro o shoji" ["the mind of Joy arises"], over and over, might have made some of you sleepy. For me, the real surprise was that I would have to go through hundreds of stages before reaching even this first stage. Reaching it was just impossible. And I wondered what it could be like after this stage, with nine more stages to follow. The first stage already seemed to have reached the ultimate condition, but then came the second and third stages and so on. It was difficult to understand what sort of "stages" are contemplated. But just in that moment, I thought of comparing them with the "Oxherding Pictures." This helped me make sense of the stages in my own way. Simply speaking, here again we see the presentation of a process which contains everything from the beginning, simultaneously with developmental stages and without those stages.

Now, contrasting the sort of world of "Juji-bon," which evokes such a sensation of unreality, with our daily lives, the two seem utterly different. But then, upon reflection, I have noticed that in fact the "Juji-bon" world is similar to the practice of psychotherapy which I have been doing for many years. I meet adolescents considered "incorrigible," or "notorious scoundrels," or people who come with "criminal" on their record, as judged by ordinary superficial consciousness. What I try to see is a realm where the deepest within the person contains everything, including change and no change. I have tried to focus on the realm beyond such discriminations as are implied in ideal like "healing the illness," "bad person becomes good," etc. Of course, during the therapy process, the change happens on the superficial level, so we need to pay respectful attention to that part. However, the greater part of my effort is spent in contact with the realm which is unrelated to the developmental changes. This attitude of mine was acquired and cultivated during my long clinical experience, as I repeated many mistakes as a result of dwelling too heavily on the scheme of developmental changes.

6. Ajase Complex

The senex-puer axis and the male-female axis play important parallel roles in the "Oxherding Pictures" and in the *Rosarium Philosophorum* series, respectively. Although, in the former series, you cannot ignore the presence of the Mother in the background, I think it is appropriate here for me to discuss the Ajase complex, as proposed by Heisaku Kozawa, an analysand of Freud, who later became a psychoanalyst in Japan. Returning to Japan after his analysis, Kozawa in 1931 wrote an essay on "Two Kinds of Guilty Conscience."[15] In that essay, to help the Japanese understand the human psyche, he proposed the "Ajase complex," which would complement Freud's Oedipus complex. The following year, he sent the German translation of this essay to Freud. Unfortunately, Freud did not respond. But I think Kozawa's idea poses a pertinent question, and a discussion of it may deepen my comparative study of these two series of pictures.

In proposing his idea, Kozawa used the legend of King Ajatasatthu [*Ajase* in Japanese] told in an early Buddhist sutra. Kozawa seems to have been following the example of Freud, who had used the Greek tragedy, *Oedipus Rex*, in developing his theory of the Oedipus complex. However, the version of the legend told by Kozawa either deliberately or accidentally differed from the story in the sutra. This is Kozawa's version of the story, in my words:

Queen Videha, wife of King Bimbasara of Magadha, was worried about losing the love of the king because of her age, declining beauty, and lack of a child. She consulted a certain prophet and learned that the sage who lived in the wood behind the palace would die in three years, reincarnate as her child, and be born as a splendid prince. However, three years was too long to wait, so she had the sage killed. Before dying, the sage spoke to her, predicting: "I will indeed enter your womb, but the child born to you will kill his father." Thus Prince Ajatasatthu [Ajase] was born. When the prince became a young man, Devadatta, an opponent of the Buddha, disclosed to Ajatasatthu his previous life as a sage. Then the prince imprisoned his father, King Bimbasara, intending to starve him to death. But as the queen secretly got food to her husband, he was able to survive. Angered by his mother's act, Ajatasatthu tried to murder her, but the prime minister intervened. Subsequently, Ajatasatthu became terribly ill with abscesses. His suffering increased until finally he was cured by the Buddha.

Based on this story, Kozawa asserts the following. Freud identified the Oedipus complex, which stems from the child's guilt over his murder of his father. In the Ajase complex, the guilt feeling is awakened by the child's redemption. Kozawa explains that the "murderous trait" in the innocent child is melted by the "self-sacrifice of the parents." This is the first time a sense of guilt emerges in the child. It is difficult to know what Kozawa means by "self-sacrifice of the parents." According to Keigo Okonogi, Kozawa's student,[16] in this story, the queen mother nurses Ajatasatthu, who is suffering in his illness. She forgives him for trying to murder her; and Ajatasatthu, empathizing with his mother's suffering, forgives her for saving the father. Consequently, the mother's love and devotion to her child cause her to forgive him. But, according to Kozawa, after this forgiveness, a sense of guilt emerges in Ajatasatthu.

In Oedipus, the vertical relation of parent-child is destroyed and changed to a horizontal son-mother, male-female relation. Then the son, after killing his father, feels guilty. In Ajatasatthu's case, the parent-child relation is retained, the focus is on the mother-son relationship. His plan to murder his mother fails, and his mother's forgiveness arouses guilt feelings within him. Since, for the Japanese, the mother-son relationship is extremely important, it is characteristic that, even without killing his mother, the son retains a strong sense of guilt.

In the background of the Oedipus story is the father-god who severely punishes sins; while in the Ajatasatthu story we find the mother-goddess who forgives all sins. One of the contributions of Jung is to interpret myths on a level beyond personal parent-child relations. He recognized the presence of activated archetypes there. In this story of Ajatasatthu, the role of the mother is primary. But when you read the Buddhist sutra, the original story does not involve the mother so much. The story in the "Nirvana Sutra" goes as follows:

Instead of the mother, it was the father, King Bimbasara, who killed the sage. Before the birth of their child, prophets in the country all had declared that this child would kill his father; therefore the queen, after giving birth, tried to kill this baby by pushing him off a high place. Rather than dying, however, he just broke a finger. When Ajatasatthu grew up, he found out about all this and starved his father to death and imprisoned his mother. He felt remorse for killing his father and suffered a high fever. This fever caused abscesses all over his body. The young king feared that, because of his great sin, he would go to hell. He heard the voice of his father, the deceased King Bimbasara, in the air encouraging him to go visit the Buddha. When he did, the Buddha explained to Ajatasatthu that his father originally had worshipped many Buddhas and that, because of his virtue, he had become king. But now his son had killed him. "If Ajatasatthu has sinned, we Buddhas also have sinned. However, since a Buddha never sins, you, Ajatasatthu, also have no sin," declared the Buddha consolingly.

As you see in the original, Ajatasatthu does kill his own father, but the murderer of the sage was the father, Bimbasara, and not the queen. There is no story in the sutra with the plot that Kozawa gives, in which the mother kills a sage in order to keep her husband's love. In the original story, we have the sage-Bimbasara relationship and then the Bimbasara-Ajatasatthu (reincarnated sage) relationship. The relationship between an old man and a youth is the important aspect. In Kozawa's version, on the other hand, the main plot has shifted to queen mother-Ajatasatthu, the mother-child relationship.

With Kozawa's disciple, Keigo Okonogi, a psychoanalyst, this shift becomes even stronger. He added the wrinkle of the queen's devotional nursing when her son was suffering from abscesses, due to his guilt over attempting to kill her: "With this silent devotion, she forgave Ajase [i.e., Ajatasatthu] of attempted murder. Then when Ajase sensed his mother's suffering, he forgave her."[17]

This sort of change happened, I believe, not through a deliberate attempt to change things. Rather, the story underwent a "cultural transformation" in the Japanese psyche. I have discussed elsewhere that, when the hidden Christians in the Edo Period tried to transmit Bible stories to people,[18] these stories underwent Japanese transformations. Here, I think, we have a similar situation.

So how could we understand this change in the story? In the sutra, only men are prominent. The Buddha, who redeems Ajatasatthu, is also a man. This redemption, however, is based upon the maternal principle, the idea being that if the young king goes to hell, then the Buddha would join him there. So a drama about men takes place with the maternal principle as background. This seems to resemble the "Ten Oxherding Pictures." There, too, a masculine drama evolved through the archetypal function of the Mother, in a circular frame. Translated to the personal level, that is the mother-son relationship.

Consequently, Kozawa and Okonogi, as psychoanalysts, take this story at the personal level and interpret it as one about the mother-child relationship. My guess is that this is why such a transformation happened. The Ajase complex was proposed by Kozawa, who emphasizes the importance of the mother-son relationship in contrast to Freud's father-son focus. In this respect, Jung similarly asserted the significance of the maternal aspect, in contrast to Freudian theory. The difference between them is that Kozawa dealt with the mother-son problem at the personal level, while Jung discussed it at the archetypal level.

While noting the dominance of the maternal principle as the background, we have recognized the masculine senex-youth relationship as the primary structure in the Ajatasatthu story. The same is true of the "Oxherding Pictures." This seems to be significant for understanding the Japanese-Chinese type of psyche, in which the senex-puer archetype is of greater importance than the male-female relationship.

In the part of the story altered by Kozawa, I think it is important to acknowledge that the reason the queen had the sage killed was to keep her husband's love. It was not out of parental love for a child. Now, to commit murder out of concern for a husband's love is quite a selfish act. A woman, however, not only possesses devotional love for her child, but also she must care about her own self, her ego needs, even if that seems selfish. In terms of individualism, her act is a step forward. I wonder if Kozawa unconsciously is trying to express his expectation of a new Japanese feminine image. Actually, many women I have met in the field of psychotherapy have been surprisingly assertive, if not selfish, trying to live more in accord with a paternal principle; while Japanese men are tied up with the maternal principle. As a result, these women's husbands and fathers have been rather weak and not quite able to confront them. As they experience such situations repeatedly these days, how are the Japanese transforming themselves?

7. "Oxherding Pictures" by a Contemporary Woman

I have mentioned a feature of some contemporary Japanese women, but this is a trend among a very small portion only, not all. In the "Oxherding Pictures," no female figure appears. Is this related to the fact that those pictures always were painted by men? It is well known that there have long been female Zen masters. But no "Oxherding Pictures" are known to have been painted by women. I have been fortunate to see a series painted by a contemporary Japanese woman.[19] She was experienced in meditation and also knew the "Oxherding Pictures." But she was not trying to transmit an "enlightenment" experience to others. Rather, she needed to draw her own series for herself while she was getting into her own individuation process. In her set, there are ten pictures which resemble Kuo-an's pictures, plus a prologue of three pieces and an epilogue of two pieces—fifteen pictures altogether. While the set is somewhat similar to Kuo-an's, I want to focus on the differences.

When you think of it, it is only women who could do such a thing in Japan. Great masters already have proposed, executed, and perfected the "Oxherding Pictures" as a model, so it would be difficult for Japanese men to draw anything different from that. They are, as has often been noted, still stuck in the system under the maternal principle. It is nearly impossible to step out of it. From that perspective, women are much freer.

In addition, the woman who drew the series clearly states that she was not trying to make another copy. These pictures are titled "For Your Own Ox, Look Around." She is saying, "I will find my own, so you find your own." It may be that, when ancient masters first painted their "oxherding" works, they felt the same way she did. Then perhaps these series solidified as models, becoming part of a long, well-preserved tradition. In contrast, this contemporary woman appeals to others: "Try to find your own ox." Then she says, "Anyway, here is mine. I'll show you this." Thus do I see the contemporary meaning of her series.

Among the pictures, I was struck by the third picture of her prologue, in which the boy, who is going out to look for the ox, actually is enclosed in a large ox. And as the background, we see the setting sun. Kuo-an's series had an ox in a circle, but in this picture the circle is enclosed in the ox. In Kuo-an's tenth picture, the ox disappears. For the tenth in

Fig. 21. "I'm fed up! This same old routine is so boring."

Fig. 22. An old man said, "Your bull has run away."

Fig. 23. "I'm wondering whether in fact I can find my bull."

Fig. 24. Setting out on my Journey into the Deep Mountain

Fig. 25. Descending into the Valley and Finding the Traces

Fig. 26. Looking deep down into my Reflections and Glimpsing my
Bull.

Fig. 27. The Struggle on the Edge of the Cliff.

Fig. 28. A Total Vision of the Way Back Home.

Fig. 29. Surrendering to my Bull, Surrendering to the Wind.

Fig. 30. The Fear of Letting Go.

Fig. 31. Dawn.

Fig. 32. The Whole World is my Home.

Fig. 33. Enticing my Friends out into the Path.

Fig. 34. The Toast of Celebration to the New Journey.

Fig. 35. Yes . . . , you have to search for your own bull yourself.

this series, two oxen appear. In addition, in the second picture of the epilogue, again an ox appears. In Kuo-an's series,
the circle had significant meaning, while in this contemporary one, the focus seems to shift to the ox.

Today, when we think of the process of self-realization or
of individuation, we tend to have an image of developmental,
linear progress toward "completion." Kuo-an, however, presented a circular image. The emphasis of this contemporary
series is on the process itself, rather than on completion.
Contemporary man, whether of East or West, cannot expect
protection from the circle. Each person is in her or his own
process of searching for her/his own ox. There is no guarantee
as to when the process will end.

This modern woman's series is in color, whereas Kuo-an's
is in black and white. Zen people, among others, say that a
sumi- [black ink] *e* [painting] includes all the colors. It must
be true that it isn't necessary to add colors. But looking at the
radiance of this fully colored eighth painting made me imagine that, if a Zen monk forgets that "*sumi-e*" means a full-
color painting, he may get lost in the radiant color used by a
woman. A Zen monk's training, of course, does not deal with
the illustration of the anima figure or with man's soul as represented by a female figure. The beautifully colored anima figure might dazzle his eyes. A rather unnecessary speculation,
perhaps.

In this modern series also, the main character is a boy,
not a girl. I asked the artist about it. "No particular reason.
The image just came up. Couldn't help it," was her answer.
Even at the present time, as far as the conception of the "Oxherding" series goes, the senex-puer axis seems significant. It
would not be easy to develop a male-female axis. In the case
of her pictures, I get the impression of a hermaphrodite or a
figure of undifferentiated gender.

Creating such pictures could be plain nonsense for a Zen
priest who has attained enlightenment. Certainly this woman
never even implied that she had done so. Nevertheless, a
woman who lives in the present time, knowing that famous

male Zen priests already had painted such pictures, tried to capture relevant images in her mind and appealed to people, one by one, to "look for your own ox."

8. Healing of the Swans

Though impressed by the "Oxherding Pictures" and having gained a lot from Buddhist teaching, I still adhere to the idea that the anima figure is a woman, because I think that our Japanese blind spot may be there. While obsessed by such a thought, I became aware of the following. In many cultures in the world, stories of swan maidens offer romantic anima images. The swan typically flies down from the sky and lands in a lake or pond, transforms herself into a young woman, and bathes. Then a certain man falls in love with her. The story then develops from there into various plots.

I want to focus on the presence or absence of such a story in a culture. I have found stories of swan maidens in the *Fudo-Ki*, a collection of stories from before the transmission of Buddhism to Japan. This work contains local history and legends of various areas that were compiled by order of an emperor in the eighth century A.D. Parts of the original compilation have been preserved until now. However, there is no swan maiden story among all the stories and fairy tales which have been told since, down through history until the present. It seems that the image of the swan maiden disappeared with the influence of Buddhism. Feeling this was regrettable, I searched everywhere to find the swan maiden in at least one story or another, but I came up with nothing.

While feeling the disappointment of this failure, I heard a case report of sandplay therapy and there finally found the image of the swan. It was the third picture of the sandplay series made by an eight-year-old girl who suffered from severe asthma.[20] Her therapist, when he saw the scene created by the child, felt very clearly, "She will get well!"

There was a small pond surrounded by trees. The child called it a spring. Three swans on it were about to take off. Around the spring were a zebra and rabbits. Flowers were arranged at the four corners. At the upper right corner, there were two girls. The child explained, saying, "This is the forest which no human beings know. This spring is the 'Healing Spring.' Tired animals are coming here. These animals were rejected by humans, but they are cared for by these two girls. The animals all get well at this spring."

It is moving to encounter a child suffering from psychosomatic illness who then is cured by making sandplay pictures. She was healed by discovering the "Healing Spring" at the innermost core of her psyche. Here I would like to keep my focus on the swan instead of the sandplay process. As soon as I saw this picture, I thought of the swan maidens who had disappeared from the Japanese psyche after the transmission of Buddhism. They were "rejected" by the Japanese, and they were tired, but not extinct. And now they are beginning to heal, deep in the hearts of young Japanese. In short, the image of the romantic anima is becoming activated in the psyche of contemporary Japanese.

It may seem strange that I am so moved by one sandplay picture made by an eight-year-old girl, after showing the "Ox-herding Pictures" made by Zen masters. To put it briefly, this reflects my belief that, for us contemporary Japanese, the "Oxherding Pictures" and the Rosarium pictures are equally important. I mentioned at the beginning that I do not practice psychotherapy according to Buddhist doctrine. Yet, after practicing psychotherapy among the Japanese, I have learned a lot from the "Oxherding Pictures." For the actual practice of psychotherapy, however, the union of masculine and feminine, as depicted in the Rosarium Philosophorum, seems very important. In those pictures, the ego's role in the individual is respected.

In the child's sandplay, the "Healing Spring" was located in the "forest which no human beings know," i.e., the greatness of nature. Contemporary man, who is so cut off from nature, heals as he regains contact with nature. But if you emphasize nature too much, the individuality of persons will diminish or disappear. In the next chapter, I shall discuss in-

dividuality in relation to how you see the relationship between human beings and nature. Human beings are part of
nature but are, in fact, endangering its very existence. It is
our task to resolve this conflict. The modern West stresses
the human, and the East always has stressed nature. In the
sandplay, there are two girls and they are even in the "forest
which no human beings know." There they are healing the
animals, helped by the power of the "Healing Spring." This
is a paradox. But in accepting such a paradox, the powers of
both nature and the human being will work in harmony. It is
interesting to see that these two at the spring are girls, not
the old man who often appears in Japanese fairy tales.

The modern Western ego feels pride in the strength of
the young, mature man. Eastern consciousness proudly shows
the old man's wisdom. This is illustrated by the old man in
the last picture of Kuo-an's series. But, I am afraid that the
old man's wisdom tends to become hardened. A modern girl
suffering from asthma chose girls rather than an old man as
the mediator in her healing process, despite paying utmost
respect to the power of nature. And maybe the swans healed
there will become swan maidens, whose existence has been
forgotten for so long. I feel they will engage in healing many
persons.

My imagination may be criticized as far out; but for me,
this sandplay picture forms a bridge between the "Oxherding
Pictures" and the *Rosarium* pictures in the heart of modern
Japanese. With Buddhism as its ground, a fresh movement is
emerging in the modern Japanese psyche. I have been able to
indicate this movement through two persons' works which
seem to me highly significant; new "Oxherding" pictures and
a girl's sandplay showing the healing of the swans. I am convinced that the role Japanese women are playing in the new
consciousness revolution is great.

Chapter 3

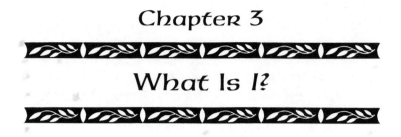

What Is *I*?

When you ask yourself, "Who am I?" I think you can easily answer with something like "I am John's father," "I am Ralph Emerson," etc. But I also think that "What is *I*?" is not easily answered.

I am italicizing this "*I*" deliberately, to indicate that it is pointing to my being as a whole. This includes everything: conscious and unconscious, my body, and perhaps other elements. It is, anyway, the *I* who stands here, everything contained in myself. So, one can say that this *I* is filled with things not ordinarily known to me.

Because of this, *I* is quite a difficult matter. Nevertheless, we ordinarily use the word "I" as if what it designates were completely self-evident. The Japanese and the English usages and their meanings of the word do differ somewhat; but in both languages, "I" is used without much reflection, without seeing that it is a complex matter. Yet, if you start thinking about *I*, the more you think, the more you find its existence becoming incomprehensible. I heard the following Buddhist story in my childhood, unforgettably.

A certain traveler happened to stay overnight in a lonely hut. In the middle of the night, a goblin came in, lugging a corpse. Almost immediately, another goblin came and argued that the corpse was his. They couldn't agree at all and finally asked the traveler for his judgment. "It belongs to the first goblin," he suggested. Exploding with anger, the second goblin ripped out the traveler's arm. Seeing that, the first one pulled an arm off the corpse and put it onto the traveler's body. The second goblin, infuriated, jerked another arm off the traveler. Again it was replaced with the corpse's other arm by the first goblin. They kept this up for awhile, and by the time the bodies of the traveler and the corpse had gotten completely exchanged, the two goblins were finally exhausted. So, they stopped fighting and ate half the corpse each. With that, they left. The shocked traveler, seeing that what apparently had been his body had been eaten up by the goblins, became confused as to whether the one now alive was really himself or not.

To my young mind, this was quite an awesome and at the same time humorous story, so I never let myself forget it. However, I could only remember this much of it, and not the conclusion, no matter how hard I tried. Eventually, I had to find a person who still owned the book, and I was able to read it. According to that book, the conclusion is as follows:

> Being terribly upset, the traveler went to talk with a monk. "Not having your body, that's nothing new," the monk commented. "The *I* of a human being is a composite of various elements. It's only temporarily formed into one thing. Foolish people, captured by this *I*, suffer a great deal. Once you know what this real *I* is, your suffering will disappear at once."[1]

With words of such deep significance even when I read it now, no wonder this ending didn't stick in a child's mind. Whether or not you agree with this Buddhist conclusion, you still will sense how difficult it is to grasp and to understand what this existence, this *I*, is.

1. Ego and I

When I have thought of *I*, I have been influenced by the Western way of thinking. When I was young, in thinking about something or studying, we relied only on the Western method. It never crossed our minds to consider the Buddhist approach to such matters. It may sound strange to Western-ers, but this is the way it generally is for Japanese.

During my student years, I read Freud with great interest. As I studied little by little, I found that the original German word, which in English is translated as *ego*, originally was written in Freud's publications as *Ich*. I was surprised. Freud describes *Ich* and *es*—that is, *I* and *it* (always translated as *ego* and *id*)—as separate elements of oneself. If I and it are separa-ble in such a way, is it possible, for example, that while *I* talk here, *it* is sleeping at my house in Japan? Ordinarily speaking, it never happens that way. *I* and *it* are always together, and the existence which includes both we call "I."

Yet, with Freud, I as a whole was divided into two. It is worth remembering here that Freud deliberately denomi-nated half of the whole I as "I" or "ego." This *Ich* [I, or ego] of Freud's probably is the same as the I of modern man and the I of Descartes' "I think; therefore, I am." Freud's contribu-tion is that he clarified ego as always threatened by the id, even though he used "I" to refer to only a part of the mind. By this we realize how much he valued that part. Therefore, even though pointing out the importance of the id, his oft-quoted phrase, "Where id was, there ego shall be,"[2] indicates clearly that the main focus was on *Ich*, on ego.

In Europe in Freud's time, it was to be expected that such a powerful "I" would build modern European culture and ex-tend it over the whole world. It is truly amazing that, in such an environment, Jung, from early in his career, asserted the significance of *Selbst* (Self) as opposed to Freud's *Ich*.

When Freud's work was translated into English, his *Ich* and *es* were given the Latin equivalents *ego* and *id*. The merit of this usage was that it became possible, when we human beings think about our own minds, to objectify a great deal.

By doing so, we are able to "analyze" the human mind. Analysis enables us to know the dynamism and structure of the human mind. Various schools of depth psychology have emerged as a result. The understanding of neurosis also has been advanced. All this occurred as psychotherapy developed.

At the same time, this selection of terms for translation created various problems. Freudian psychoanalyst Bruno Bettelheim initially criticized the use of the Latin words[3] as bringing psychoanalysis too close to the medical model, giving the impression that analysts were observing the patient's mind objectively. As a result, psychoanalysis became broadly accepted in the United States. Only recently have the problematical aspects of this orientation become noticeable. People seemed to forget that psychoanalysis had begun with *Ich*, self-analysis, and too much emphasis was placed on trying to manipulate the patient.

In chapter 1, I pointed out that depth psychology originated in Freud's and Jung's self-analysis. Such self-analysis is not a matter of applying the laws of natural science. Unfortunately, the use of such terms as *ego* and *id* caused people to mistake this psychology for a branch of natural science.

Would it be better to use "I" to express all of me, instead of distinguishing between ego and id, or between Jung's ego and unconscious? It might be more correct but less effective in terms of thinking about problems of the human mind. Thinking about the human mind and about existence is very difficult. It is effective to think of the mind as divided, but that is not the reality. It may be more correct to think of it as a whole, but you cannot go anywhere with that definition, as it is difficult to discuss the structure of the psyche if everything is "I."

Nonetheless, you can say that thinking of ego and I as identical reflects very clearly the mode of modern Western thought. In contrast to this, then, I shall consider the questions: How do Japanese think? How does Buddhism think?

2. I Am a Kannon

The story given below indicates the medieval Japanese view of "I." This story, from a collection of Buddhist fables called *Konjaku Monogatari*,[4] edited in the twelfth century, A.D., is one of my favorites. First I would like to comment briefly on Buddhist tales in that era. After Buddhism was transmitted to Japan in the sixth century, it spread quickly. Among the general population, however, it was not well understood, as its doctrines, rules, and rituals were totally unfamiliar. Instead, Buddhism was received to the extent that it fused with Shinto, the indigenous animistic religion, and gradually it came to permeate daily life.

Buddhist monks, by explaining the sutras and teaching the doctrines, on the one hand, and by telling many illustrative stories, on the other, transmitted the values of Buddhism. These stories recounted true episodes and also legends containing Buddhist teachings. Many of these, collected in the Middle Ages, have been preserved. Reading them, I have felt that the nature of the Buddhism which the Japanese accepted was more readily grasped in these stories than in the sutras per se. I was glad to learn that William LaFleur, professor of Japanese studies at the University of Pennsylvania, also holds this view.[5] This story from *Konjaku Monogatari* is called "Wato Kannon in Shinano, Taking the Tonsure":

> A man living in a village with a medicinal hot spring had a dream in which someone said, "Tomorrow about 2 p. m., Kannon [Kuan Yin], the Bodhisattva of Compassion, will arrive at this hot spring." He was surprised and asked what appearance the Kannon would have. Someone said, "A samurai of about forty years, on horseback," and went on describing his appearance in detail. Then the man woke up. He told everybody in the village. They cleaned the area and then gathered at the spring to welcome the Bodhisattva. Two o'clock passed. About four o'clock in the afternoon, a samurai exactly matching the description appeared. Everyone prostrated themselves before him. The samurai, perplexed, asked, "What's

going on?" A monk told him about the dream oracle. The samurai explained that he had fallen from his horse and injured himself and that was why he had come to the hot spring. But the villagers kept praying. The samurai said, "Then, I must be Kannon," and he took the tonsure on the spot. It is said that, following this, he went up to Mount Hiei, near Kyoto, and became a disciple of the priest Kakucho.[6]

The most impressive aspect of the story for me is that the samurai believes "I must be Kannon," on the basis of a stranger's dream. Abandoning his forty-year life as a warrior, he is convinced that "I am Kannon" and becomes a priest. If I take Descartes' maxim, "I think; therefore, I am," and express this situation, it becomes "Someone dreamed of me; therefore, I exist."

One might well think that this is just nonsense. But Jungians might remember the dream that Jung described from his later years:

> I was on a hiking trip. I was walking along a little road through a hilly landscape; the sun was shining and I had a wide view in all directions. Then I came to a small wayside chapel. The door was ajar, and I went in. To my surprise there was no image of the Virgin on the altar, and no crucifix either, but only a wonderful flower arrangement. But then I saw that on the floor in front of the altar, facing me, sat a yogi—in lotus posture, in deep meditation. When I looked at him more closely, I realized that he had my face. I started in profound fright, and awoke with the thought: "Aha, so he is the one who is meditating me. He has a dream, and I am it." I knew that when he awakened, I would no longer be.[7]

Upon reading this, you see that Jung also used another's dream to answer the question, "What am I?" The yogi dreams, and Jung is supported by the yogi's dreaming. Therefore, the sentence, "Someone dreamed me; therefore, I am," seems to fit. There is, of course, a clear difference between Jung's case and that of the samurai in medieval Japan. In Jung's case, the yogi is a character in his own dream, and, as Jung relates, "he had my face." In his comment, Jung states, "It is a parable." In contrast, for the samurai in that era, the dream was someone else's; and he, the character who had been dreamed of, accepted the content as literal reality. Jung commented on his own dream as follows:

> The aim of [this dream] is to effect a reversal of the relationship between ego-consciousness as the generator of the empirical personality. This reversal suggests that, in the opinion of the "other side," our unconscious existence is the real one and our conscious world a kind of illusion, an apparent reality constructed for a specific purpose, like a dream which seems a reality as long as we are in it. It is clear that this state of affairs resembles very closely the Oriental conception of Maya.

Here, Jung recognizes his own dream experience as being similar to "the Oriental" view. Considering these aspects, I get the impression that Jung's *I* existed astride both Japan's Middle Ages and the modern Occident. When you think about what *I* is, in the contemporary West, ego is equal to *I*. Jung, who questioned that equation, began at the ego and descended to the depths of the mind. In contrast, the medieval Japanese *I* did not discriminate itself from others and accepted an existence which fused self and other. But, modern Japanese, including myself, are trying to find *I* as more individual and are rising toward the light of discrimination. I met the Occident in the field of analytical psychology.

Jung's psychology is quite deep and expansive, so, in order to accept it, Westerners have tried to understand it in relation to ego. In contrast, I have observed that Japanese or Asians in general have tried to understand its relation to the Being itself before the division of self and other.

3. *I in the Dream*

It is well worth considering the active I in dreams when we think about the nature of *I*. Obviously, this includes not only

I in my own dream, but also myself in another's dream. There-fore, I am aware of my dream; and also, as a therapist, I am attentive to the appearance of myself in my analysands' dreams. The latter give insight into various points of "what *I* am." Here is one example. Near the termination of therapy, a school-phobic high school student dreamed as follows:

> I come to Sensei's [therapist's] house, but there is no response, so I go around to the back. In the backyard, people are sitting in a half circle. They look like stone Jizo Bodhisattva [the guardian deity of children]. In the front row, there are chil-dren, and behind them are adults. Looking more carefully, I see that there are people sitting the same way in the living room. In the center, Sensei is lying down. (The half-circle of people gives the strong impression of being half in the light and half in darkness) I yell loudly from the back, "I am here," or "I got here on time," but no response. Soon Sensei stands up and tries to say something, but no sound comes out. Every-body pushes him back and makes him lie down. The whole scene looked like the picture of the Buddha's Nirvana (i.e., his passing away while entering Nirvana).

This client thought of this last scene as the death of his thera-pist, so he hesitated in telling me about it, thinking that it might indicate bad fortune, but finally he told me. Actually, I have "died" several times in clients' dreams. In almost all of them, this was dreamed near the termination point of ther-apy. As a Jungian analyst, of course, one does not think of a death dream as "bad fortune." In the therapeutic process, the experience of "death and rebirth" manifests itself to the client as well as to the therapist in dreams. This dream occurred close to termination and thus indicated transformation not only of the *image* of the therapist, but also of the therapist himself—of me, in this case. That is, it meant that some transformation already had taken place, or was going to take place, within me.

The significance of the initial dream has always been pointed out. You can also say that termination dreams have special significance. The above dream indicates that the therapist has finished his role and is leaving. This client and I then discussed this. He too felt that the therapy had nearly reached the end. At this point, we both felt that it was quite interesting that, although both of us were completely indifferent to Buddhism, the significant Buddhist image, the Buddha's Nirvana, appeared.

At that time, I did not give any more thought to the dream. I focused on the idea that the dream indicated a change in his image of the therapist. But when I look back on it now, I believe that the dream was referring to my reality as well. I feel that this dream was indicating how much weight Buddhism exerts on the way I conduct psychotherapy, even though at that time I was not ready consciously to accept the fact. I saw the dream's half-light and half-dark field of people surrounding the central figure in terms of the client's work on his "shadow" problem. Now I see that it may have indicated my own half-conscious state of mind as regards Buddhism.

In my own dreams, my *I* does things that would be completely out of character for the *I* in the awake state. In one's dream, sometimes the *I* becomes not oneself but another, or an animal, a plant, or even an inorganic being. There is an old story from a dream in which the *I* becomes an animal:

> There was a man who hunted birds with falcons. He lived with his wife and three children and kept many falcons and dogs for hunting. He was getting quite old, and one night he was feeling sick but not able to fall asleep. Finally, near dawn, he fell asleep and had a dream. He and his family were pheasants living happily in the meadow. Suddenly, hunters, with falcons diving and dogs charging, started after them. Right there in front of his eyes, his wife and three sons were murdered in cold blood by the falcons. When he saw he would be next, he woke up.
>
> He began to think about all the many pheasants he had killed. Those pheasants must have felt as sad as he felt in the

dream. So he let all his falcons and dogs loose. In tears, he told this dream to his wife and children. Immediately he re-nounced the world and took the tonsure.[8]

I have summarized the story for you, but the original contains a lively and detailed description of how frightened the hunter/pheasant became, witnessing his wife and children be-ing murdered in front of him. This shows how well he had re-experienced the sadness of pheasants in the dream.

The notable characteristic of this story is that, in the dream, the dreamer became a being other than human and by that gained empathy toward pheasants. Then this *I*'s expe-rience in the dream became the generator of its behavior in the waking state. This type of thing happens in varying de-grees in my practice of analysis at the present time. The cases of becoming an animal in dreams are rare, but they do exist in Japan. There may be fewer in Europe and America, but I wonder.

You sometimes see yourself doing something in a dream—for example, you see yourself falling from a high place. In a dream you might clearly experience your "double." In a dream, you might meet another you. The phenomenon of the "double" was long considered abnormal. Goethe and the French poet Alfred de Musset experienced it. But, in dream, although it is not common, it is not considered patho-logical. This phenomenon is interesting in terms of learning about *I*, so I decided to collect cases and present an essay on it. Then I had a dream of my "double." A short one, it had a strong impact:

> I was walking down the hallway next to a psychiatric hospital. Then, I saw myself clearly there, wearing an ochre-colored sweater (one which, in fact, I wear often), sitting as though waiting for an appointment. I passed by. Then I had a feeling of surprise: This must be a dream of a double! I awoke think-ing that the one who was walking was wearing a navy blue sweater.

To do "research" on dreams of the double sounds somewhat like looking on from outside. But to dream such a dream
myself and, in addition, to see that the "other me" obviously
was waiting to be examined as a patient—these aspects
struck my heart strongly. The one walking down the hallway
was there in a "therapist" role. The other half of my self was
a "patient." Both of them came together there.

Adolph Guggenbuhl-Craig discusses the healer archetype
in his book, *Power in the Helping Professions.*[9] Any archetype
includes opposite elements, e.g., therapist/patient, healer/
healed. Thus Guggenbuhl-Craig affirms that this opposition
exists in the healer archetype. If, despite that, a therapist defines herself or himself as a "healthy person without ailment,"
this archetype gets split away and the therapist becomes
just a therapist and the patient just a patient. Sadly, the patient then loses the opportunity of healing the self through
the functioning of the healer archetype. In order to prevent
such a splitting off of the archetype, the therapist first has
to recognize the patient that exists within herself or himself.
Therefore, meeting myself as a patient in that dream was
meaningful to me in carrying on my work as a psychotherapist.

Having little awareness of "the patient," I actually became a patient in my own dream. Experiencing the encounter
of the therapist-self with the patient-self was significant in
reinforcing my consciousness of our fundamental coexistence. To "Who am I?," I can answer, "I am a psychotherapist." But the answer to the question, "What is *I?*," must be
"I am a psychotherapist and at the same time a patient." Isn't
it wonderful that a dream can actually make one feel this!

4. The World of Hua-yen

I have mentioned that *I* am a therapist as well as a patient.
Recollecting the dreams I have presented so far, I can also say
that *I* am an animal as well as Kannon. In a psychotherapy
session, quite often I feel myself sitting as a stone or a patient
or Kannon, rather than as a "therapist," and I think it has a

better result. So I easily becomes this or that. Then, if I were asked afresh, "What is *I?*" what could I say?

While I was preoccupied with the above ideas, I encountered the world of the *Garland Sutra*. As I have said, it is very difficult to read this sutra. So, I just keep reading, half-sleeping and skimming, on and on. But, when I enter that world in such a manner, even without comprehending each meaning and relationship, I get the feeling that I am enveloped in light. I am immersed in the feeling. Sometimes you see amazing words, but if you are absentminded, you will just pass on, continuing to read as if they are nothing special. For example: "Every act is empty; no reality; ordinary people think it is real; all things, no self-nature, all, completely equal to nothingness."

As explained above, "no self-nature" is important among the teachings in the *Garland Sutra*. Until now, I have been persistent in asking, "What is *I?*" According to the *Garland Sutra*, my essence, my unique nature, is nothing, nonexistent. So this question makes no sense. This is quite a radical idea.

As I continued reading the sutra, I felt, "This is really something! What am I going to do?" It was so vague and impossible to grasp. Although I could not think that "my unique nature" does not exist, it started to give me the feeling that my nature is but a drop of water in the ocean. Luckily, I found an essay in English on the *Garland Sutra* by the Japanese philosopher, Toshihiko Izutsu.[10] Thanks to him, I shall explain briefly the principal ideas of this sutra.

This sutra calls the world of ordinary life "the Dharmic World of Phenomena." Its condition is such as we ordinarily experience when there are two separate things, A and B. A has its own particular characteristics, as does B; A and B thus are clearly distinguished from one another, and there is no question of confusing the two. If the boundaries between phenomena are removed, however, we see the world differently. This dissolution of boundaries is characteristic not only of *Hua-yen (Kegon)*, but also of Buddhism in general and other Eastern philosophies. "The minute and infinite differences of actual existence instantly disappear in a vast space of nondiscrimination."[11] This world of Hua-yen is called "the Dharmic World of Principle."

Here, the differences between objects disappear, and so self-nature is negated. This state Zen Buddhism calls "nothingness or emptiness"; the *Garland Sutra* uses the term "absolute emptiness." Everything is "non-self-nature" [*nihsvabhava*]. Such terms as "nothingness" and "emptiness" do not signify an empty world of no things, but rather a world that contains infinite possibilities for "being." "Emptiness" in the Dharmic World of Principle is pregnant with the dual meaning of nothingness and being.

According to Dr. Izutsu, in order to have such "emptying" of existence, the same process of emptying existence has to happen on the side of the consciousness of the subject which is viewing it . In short, it is necessary to empty our ordinary consciousness, our "discriminating mind," which discriminates things one from another, always wanting to see the differences. "It is the prerequisite. 'Emptying' consciousness is the precondition for emptying existence."[12] The world of the Principle, which is itself absolutely emptied and hence infinitely potential, self-divides into innumerable phenomenal forms, the world we call "reality." The Principle manifests into the phenomena. This kind of manifestation of the Emptiness Principle is predicated in Hua-yen philosophy as "the Arising of True Nature." The most important point of the arising is complete manifestation. That is, the Principle, as Emptiness, always manifests itself completely in its appearance as form. Each and everything which can be said to belong to our world of experience manifests this principle wholly and without exception. Even small things—a flower in a field, a single speck of dust floating in the air—manifest this creative energy totally.

The world of phenomena embodies various kinds of discrimination. Each and every thing can be seen separately. But once a person acknowledges their Emptiness before or beneath such discrimination, one can see the world entirely nondiscriminately. Everything exists in the principle: "All things manifest in the Arising of True Nature." Dr. Izutsu comments:

> The Principle permeates phenomena without the slightest hindrance and is thus none other than the phenomena themselves. Conversely, phenomena manifest the Principle without the least obstruction and are thus none other than the Principle itself. The Principle and phenomena are tracelessly interfused and mutually interpenetrating. This relationship between Principle and phenomena is termed in Hua-yen philosophy, "the Mutual Interpenetration of Principle and Phenomena."[13]

Having presented the important concepts in Hua-yen philosophy of the Dharmic World of Phenomena, the Dharmic World of Principle, and the Dharmic World of the Mutual Interpenetration of Principle and Phenomena, I shall now introduce a final formulation, by which the development of Hua-yen's theory of existence reaches its innermost core. It can be termed "the Mutual Interpenetration of Phenomena and Phenomena."

5. Interdependent Origination [Prati tya-samutpada]

I have mentioned that the Principle always manifests itself completely in its appearance in form. Each of these forms is a different existence; the Principle is their utter nondiscrimination, i.e., there are separate things, A, B, C, and these are all "non-self-nature." Is this possible? Hua-yen answers in two ways.

In preparation, I shall introduce the idea of "ontological nexus" in Hua-yen philosophy. Suppose there are the phenomena A, B, and C, and each of them is itself without any self-nature, yet they all are related. Consequently, the existence of A as "A" is determined by its relation to B and C and all other phenomena. Everything is related to everything; nothing can be considered apart from its relatedness to the whole. Dr. Izutsu has skillfully presented this visually with the aid of a diagram. This figure, however, attempts to diagram the structure of the mutual relationships among all entities in a single instant. As any thing moves in time or space, all things will change in relationship to it. Although A is without self-nature, still it is A because of its relationship to everything else. In short, the inner structure of A includes everything else in hidden or "powerless" form. And by such relationship, A is A, not B or C.

The entire universe supports the existence of any single thing, and absolutely nothing exists as an individual particular by itself alone. All things continually and simultaneously manifest themselves together as a whole. The philosophy of the Hua-yen calls this ontological reality "Interdependent Origination." The Arising of True Nature and Interdependent Origination are the key concepts of Hua-yen thought. Nagarjuna said, "Whoever sees Interdependent Origination can see Emptiness." As no "individual" can exist in itself alone, it exists by the support of everything other than itself. Through everything, one indivisible Principle exists—in short, the Mutual Interpenetration of Phenomena and Phenomena.

The way of thought of Interdependent Origination has a nature completely different from the conceptual mode of Aristotle, which explains phenomena by the relationship of cause and effect. Although modern science, utilizing the cause-and-effect point of view regarding phenomena, has proven extremely effective, we need to reflect upon the modern problems that stem from our habit of viewing all manmade phenomena in a cause-and-effect mode. It seems quite worthwhile to look at these problems from the standpoint of Interdependent Origination. Jung's concept of synchronicity belongs to the thought pattern of Interdependent Origination.

One other idea, an ontology of "master and servant," is needed in order to explain the Dharmic World of the Mutual Interpenetration of Phenomena and Phenomena. Suppose that there are entities A, B, and C, each differing from the other. Each in turn, according to Hua-yen, is constituted by an indefinite number of the same ontological elements, a, b, c, d, e, f, g, . . . , even though A, B, and C differ. If we use semantic thinking, the signifier is always everything (a, b, c . . .), whereas the significants differ, like A, B, C.

In order to explain this enigma, Hua-yen employs the aspects "powerful" and "powerless." "Powerful" designates the presence of a positive, manifest, self-asserting, and controlling element; "powerless" denotes the opposite: passive, seclusive, self-negating, and subservient. Among the infinite elements, one of them—a, l, or x, perhaps—becomes "powerful," while the rest of them are understood to be "powerless." Then, as A, L, or X, they are recognized in the daily world as different things. This is the concept of an ontology of "master and servant." At any one moment, the powerful element is not necessarily the only one; and it changes in relation to the whole and over time.

As explained above, A, B, and C will be recognized as different from each other, but that is due to the relationships of the constituting elements, both powerful and powerless. When you pay complete attention to the constituting elements, all entities are embraced in profound samadhi. This is the Mutual Interpenetration of Phenomena and Phenomena. In our daily life, only the "powerful" element manifests, so we human beings cannot resist focusing on differences; that means not noticing the "powerless" elements, though they are essential to the depth-structure of A, for instance, and support its manifestation.

With this bit of familiarity with the idea of the Interpenetration of Phenomena and Phenomena, when we reconsider I, we can deepen our understanding.

6. Level of Consciousness
When you apply this understanding of Hua-yen, I then is basically empty; so my self-nature, my true quality, doesn't exist in itself. And also, I am not only others, I am similarly ani-

mals, plants, and all other things organic and inorganic. But, in order to experience the emptiness of existence, the conscious side of the subject who views must have become empty. This relates deeply to the nature of human consciousness. In terms of thinking about *I*, my consciousness is the focal point.

From early times, Buddhists were interested in human consciousness. They have practiced meditation as their method of training, and they have engaged in careful self-observation on changes in consciousness during meditation. This sort of work is practiced not only by Hua-yen adherents. Other sects of Buddhism, as well as Taoism and shamanism, have similar practices. Indeed, they are common to every religion in East and Southeast Asia.

In daily consciousness, it is important to see the differences in things. By doing so, you can discriminate usefully. Through finer and more accurate discrimination, science develops. Natural science requires increasing refinement of the ordinary consciousness. With the development of natural science and technology, we humans became capable of manipulating our environment in nearly any way our hearts desire.

Buddhism has refined its way of consciousness in a different direction. It has moved in the direction of negating the use of consciousness for discrimination between things. In an image, I might say "gradually lowering" the level of consciousness or gradually annihilating discrimination. When you lower it to an extreme degree—that is, when consciousness becomes emptied—the world manifested is that presented in the *Garland Sutra*, as we have seen. You might say that the lowered level of consciousness means the "unconscious." But, as Jung noted, "the characteristic of the unconscious is not being able to be conscious." Therefore, the so-called "unconscious," as long as you can talk about it, actually is conscious. The modern West has thought ego so important that it identifies itself as "I." So, as an Asian, I guess that, in regard to this "lower" consciousness, it was impossible to say "conscious," since the modern Western ego does not comprehend this aspect. Thus this "lower" consciousness can't help but be called the "unconscious."

There is a most important point to be kept in mind regarding this descent of the level of consciousness. It does not necessarily imply a lowering of the power of conscious judgment, concentration, observation, etc. In the modern West, this has not been understood. Because the West emphasized the ego so much, all lowering of the level of consciousness was considered "abnormal" or "pathological." Carl Jung is the person who made the greatest effort to correct such an idea. From the beginning, he pointed out that regression not only has a pathological side, but also has a constructive and creative role. His experience of "Confrontation with the Unconscious," described in his autobiography, is indeed such an example of the descent of the level of consciousness with the full faculties of judgment, concentration, and observation intact. Active imagination, which he developed, was considered to be one of the powerful methods of constructively lowering the level of consciousness.

Jung has separated the "personal unconscious" and the Collective Unconscious as strata deep in the mind. They represent, if expressed in the Buddhist way, the gradual deepening of the level of consciousness. Jung made no mention of a level of "Emptiness." However, Jung's statement "The psyche is the world pivot"[14] may be taken as representing in Western terms the level of the ultimate state of nondiscrimination or emptiness. I think the reason such a big gap has emerged between Eastern and Jungian terminology for such consciousness is that Jung was protecting his position as a "psychologist" while still trying to relate to this "Emptiness." Moreover, Jung's work, fundamentally, consisted of caring for the ego. I recall Jung's frequent reminder that he does not speak about God Himself, but rather, as a psychologist, talks about images of God in the human psyche. Jung, as psychologist, limited his work to considering those things which can be grasped by ego and then verbalized. He expressed these from the ego's side, so he talked about the "personal unconscious" and the "Collective Unconscious."

Buddhism, on the other hand, passed through such an area at once and reached the level of "emptiness consciousness" or "conscious nondiscrimination." Thus it describes the consciousness from that side, not from the ego's side. In order to accomplish such a descent in level of consciousness, Buddhism developed various methods of meditation and chanting, practices which maintain full awareness of concentration and observation. The results of such effort are described in many sutras. So, during such practice as *zazen* [Zen meditation], for example, Zen refuses to attend to the "middle zone" of ego consciousness, reaching instead toward "emptiness consciousness." Jungian psychology, it seems to me, focuses on images for that middle zone, which Zen practitioners pass through, and interprets them in relation to the ego.

With this key difference in mind, I would like to discuss how I think about and practice psychotherapy. Since I was trained as a Jungian analyst, I believe that, generally speaking, I follow Jung's ideas. I also want to make it clear that I have never had an experience such as what is called "emptiness consciousness." Yet I also, at this point, don't think that I should practice Zen in order to have such an experience. Despite that, I could not help but pay attention to Buddhism, because my ego started to change, getting closer to Buddhist views. Even though I thought I was practicing psychotherapy according to Jung's ideas, probably I still have a different kind of ego from that of Westerners. Compared to the Western ego, the Japanese ego is living far more "in everything," much as I have described in presenting Hua-yen ideas. Before asserting my ego's independence and integration, I think of myself as an existence living in the world of Interdependent Origination. Frankly, when I meet those Jungian analysts who "analyze" and "interpret" everything, I feel like saying to them, "Everything is Emptiness," although I really don't comprehend what that statement means. One consequence of having such an ambiguous way of life is that

I have obtained a good number of excellent results through psychotherapy in Japan. But what I am doing need not be limited only to Japan. I hope that it also will be helpful to some degree in other cultural regions. Because this contemporary period is a time of cultural collision, I think that no one can live comfortably in their indigenous, traditional culture.

7. What Is Individuality?

As human beings, each of us thinks of herself or himself as a unique being, different from all others. Placing such a high value on individuality has happened only in this modern era in the West. There it has come to be considered extremely important to develop individuality. When such an idea came to Japan, modern Japanese also agreed with it. But here I would like to ask again what the uniqueness of individuality is, as until now we have been discussing *I*.

Basically, I think, modern European ideas are involved already when you use the word *individuality* in English to imply that each person is unique. Consequently, when you use the term *individuality* in English discussion, you are already influenced by modern European individualism, without realizing it. So, I temporarily use *individuality* for what is based on individualism, and I use *eachness* (or perhaps *selfness*) for what is based on Buddhist ideas, to distinguish between these two assumptions about persons.

The word *individual* is a negative form of *divide*, indicating "not divided." So, it is the final unit after dividing as far as you can. You can divide it no further. An individual is thus a thing that cannot be divided. *Divide* is the operative word. Now I would like you to remember Jung's strata of consciousness. That is, you can see how the function of "dividing" consciousness has been valued and refined in the West. By contrast, in Buddhist cultures, effort was spent to refine the consciousness which would *eliminate* "division," i.e., discrimination. Consequently, when you think of uniqueness in Buddhism, it must be a different idea from that of the individual of the West, so it cannot be expressed by using the word *individuality*.

The premise of modern individuality is to establish the ego first. In the young adult stage, ego will be the existence which is independent of others and equipped with initiative and integration. Reaching adulthood means that you have established your own identity. Ego which is established in such a manner will develop one's individuality, following one's own desire, judgment, and responsibility. In comparison with this, the idea of the process of *individuation*, as developed by Jung, is epoch-making. Yet Jung emphasized the importance of establishing a strong ego as its precondition. So it is clear that, in the Western world, education from childhood is geared toward developing such an independent ego.

Human beings in Buddhism, as so well clarified by Hua-yen thought, exist in relationship. When taken out of relationship, a person loses "self-nature" and thus ceases to exist. Not having "self-nature," how can the person have eachness (selfness)? We have considered the ideas of the Arising of True Nature and also Interdependent Origination. Accordingly, if one tries to respect one's own eachness, one has to be aware of others before contemplating her/his own "independence." This sort of attitude will be seen and criticized from the individualistic perspective as other-oriented and certainly quite dependent, if not "co-dependent," a fearsome state. In fact, in such relationship, one indeed can realize one's eachness, but I would like you to pay attention to the different way of thinking which lies behind this view.

Reflecting the above on the level of daily life, for example, there are many ways of saying the first person singular in Japanese. We quite naturally use the suitable form according to the situation, i.e., the relationship. We use one "I" in our family, a different one when speaking with a same-gender friend, and another when speaking publicly. The way the "I" is used communicates how the person perceives the relationship. It is the same in using the second person forms. In German, of course, "*Sie*" and "*du*" are used, while in English you can use the pronoun "you" or simply a name when addressing a person. But I think there are no examples of so many kinds of "I" in the Western languages of today.

The individual based on individualism has such clarity about her or his being, you might think that the type of each-ness not based on individualism is too vague and worthless. I myself find that both the Western individual and the Eastern eachness have their own advantages and disadvantages. I feel like saying, in accord with Buddhist ideas, always pay atten-tion to the relationship with the whole. But, in addition, you cannot actively assert "self-nature" when you have neither eachness nor initiative.

Now I would like to examine this point, applying the idea of "master and servant." Suppose that "I," for example, con-sist of a, b, c . . . an infinite number of elements; and, among them, factors b, f, and k are "powerful" elements to make "I" express "my" eachness. So, if I exert those powerful factors actively, I may cause my existence to stand out, and, by so doing, I may be able to control others. But if I think it through a little more, then actually I may die without being aware of my other infinite "powerless" elements. But if I were to live my eachness fully, I would be receptive, reclusively waiting. Then, when my "powerless" elements became acti-vated, I would discover an eachness that is different from what I had known about myself until then. In short, I would appreciate with surprise the autonomous emergence of each-ness. This has quite a different feeling from creating one's in-dividual nature by one's own effort.

In individualism, it seems quite reasonable that one develops individuality by following one's own intentions. However, little possibility exists to develop in a direction un-expected from what one already knows about oneself, as I have explained in relation to the "powerless" elements. Such development is active and positive, to be sure, but you would have to say that it is restricted by the ego's judgment. In com-parison, the Buddhist approach seems to be fulfilled if your path opens up in an unexpected direction. However, it becomes doubtful whether you can call it *eachness* when one basically is being tossed about by environmental forces.

This is one reason why I said that both the idea of Western individualism and the idea of Buddhist eachness have advantages and disadvantages. In order to compensate for their respective disadvantages, a person following the Buddhist way, while living in the fullness of Interdependent Origination, needs to hold firmly to, or live in, the consciousness that "this is I"; while a person following the Western way sometimes needs to have the courage to let go of the ego's judgment. You can say that a person has something of an identity, but, in fact, it's impossible to "establish identity," if you reflect on it thoroughly. As for the question, "What is *I?*" I would respond that, by approaching and responding to the world around me, my *I* takes its forms. For instance, now I'm finding here in Texas this sort of Kawai who was imagined only vaguely last week in Japan by that Kawai who now is recalled only dimly.

8. Suicide

In this last section concerned with contemplating *I*, I shall offer some thoughts on suicide. Suicide means: "I am capable of and decide to kill myself," or "I happen to kill myself." As a psychotherapist, this is quite relevant, since we do meet persons who attempt suicide or have strong suicidal tendencies. Sometimes during the course of therapy, a client may feel the wish to die or commit suicide.

During the process of psychotherapy, just as symbolic death and rebirth manifest themselves, so, in the process of the transformation of personality, there often emerges the constellation of mysterious "death." It may manifest as the death of parents or an acquaintance, an unexpected accident, a death experience in a dream, etc. We must be very attentive and careful about such a phenomenon and its total constellation and meaning. During such a period, the client's suicide can become a serious question or task. Some will plan their suicide or simply say, "I want to die," "It's no use living any longer," or "Everything will go well if I am gone." Another person might declare, "On such and such a date, I will commit suicide." Especially when people suffer from depression, suicide characteristically comes up.

At such times, I respect the client's experience of symbolic death and rebirth, and, to avoid actual death, I wish for the completion of the experience of the symbolic death. I take such a position to care for the client. Therefore, I do not oppose the client's wish to die. From the beginning, I listen to the client as carefully as I can. If and when that wish establishes a definite connection to actual death, then I oppose it. In such a painful process, I was deeply moved by the client's experience of death and rebirth. One client who attempted suicide later said, "Unless I had gone through being near death, I would not have been transformed." This certainly impressed me.

While I was writing chapter 1, I read David Rosen's *Transforming Depression.*[15] In the book, he discusses this idea similarly and in detail, introducing the key concept, "egocide." I was glad to see him clarify the core issue of the problem accurately. Suicide is really intended as egocide. But the client does not recognize that fact, so he tries to end his own life. The therapist's role in this connection is to clarify the core issue. In order to elucidate his theory, Rosen helpfully presents four cases.

I have not done any statistical research, nor have I seen any research papers on the topic, but I wonder if Japanese clients have more of a tendency to plan suicide or to express such an intention than their Western counterparts. When dealing with this issue, it seems most helpful to have Rosen's concept of egocide.

Even in Japanese cases, suicide probably is often egocide. Western psychology may have the hypothesis that Japanese people will commit suicide more often than Westerners, because of their relatively weak egos. But it is useful to consider the example of the recent Kobe earthquake. Even at the time of such a catastrophe, looting did not occur, and people kept order despite the scarcity of material goods. Noting such facts, we cannot hastily attribute them to the ego's weakness. Indeed, Western specialists who came after the quake were impressed by the strength of those people's "power of endurance." How can we explain the concept of egocide with such apparently conflicting facts?

Here as elsewhere, the Japanese form of ego is the focal issue. This ego has the premise of connection with others. However, it is not about the relationship of an independent ego to others. It is instead a pervasive sort of connection that exists before the ego state, a connection in which the participants share mutually the deep "empty" world. As long as a person holds such a sense of interconnectedness, then he or she has the capacity for strong endurance. But, if one loses this sense of connectedness, one's total vulnerability is exposed. The immense problem is that the existing world, which is the foundation of interconnectedness, is described as "empty" or "nothing," and at the same time as an infinite, "non-empty" world.

In general, the Japanese have a tendency to sense that the ego should be subordinate to something which transcends it, even if it is unconscious. There is a tendency to sacrifice ego for "something." In addition, if that "something" is literal nothingness, egocide seems to be easily mistaken for suicide.

In Japan, many clients say, "I'd like to die." The shock is quite strong, and it is often repeated. So the therapist eventually feels almost like saying, "Well, if you want to die so much, do as you wish!" Somehow the reiteration gradually gets to the therapist, and it is hard to bear while still trying to support such a client. So the therapist too comes to feel almost like dying. If the therapist identifies too fully with the feeling of the client, even if that client dies, the therapist may not experience the death as tragic or even important.

In one case, this sort of suffering was endured, and the

client gradually regained the power to live. Several years later, this person told me that there was no other way than to say, "I want to die," in order to express the wish to live. This one thought has taught me a great deal.

What a client says is dependent on the quality of the relationship between therapist and client. In this relationship with me, the client actually expressed her wish to live by saying, "I want to die." She could use only such words. If I had had a deeper understanding of her, maybe a different expression would have been possible. By saying, "I want to die," one gets closer to the world of "Nothingness." And I think she had no other way to express her suffering at experiencing egocide. In Japan, when you feel the existence of your connectedness with others, you can live. But egocide necessarily changes the connectedness abruptly. The change will be felt as the loss of connectedness; therefore, suicide will be attempted.

At first, I did not understand the above issues. Therefore, I was trying to prevent client suicide by a Western-style ego-to-ego connection. As a result, I was exhausting myself and still not getting a positive outcome. I should have put my effort into the relationship of my ego and Emptiness, a vertical relationship, instead of into the horizontal ego-ego (client-therapist) relationship. Since these experiences, my attitude has changed a great deal.

In the problem of suicide, a point which attracts argument among therapists is whether it is reasonable for a human being to choose her/his own death at the terminal stage of the individuation process. Unfortunately, I cannot speak from experience. I have not been in the situation in which I went with a certain person through the process of individuation and then accepted wholeheartedly the client's choice of death. I have never encountered this.

Indirectly I heard this characteristic story about the Zen master Gempo Yamamoto, whom I greatly respected. In his ninety-sixth year, after saying, "I would like to draw the curtain on my comedy in this world," Yamamoto stopped eating and died in three days. This made me think that, at the finale of the individuation process, choosing one's own death is a possibility. But I am ending this chapter unable to state clearly "Yes" or "No."

Chapter 4

Personal and Impersonal Relationships in Psychotherapy

The foundation of psychotherapy is, I believe, reliance upon the client's self-healing power. Although relying on that power, you cannot, however, simply say, "Then let the client take care of himself," because there are many difficulties along the way. One difficulty is this "self-healing power," which includes in its background the "individuation process," as Jung termed it. The direction of the force driving the process of individuation often takes one into difficulties which the ego can hardly accept. Another difficulty is the fact of the client's coming for psychotherapy, which means that the client's self-healing power is not functioning optimally. So the problem is: how do you understand the situation, and how do you proceed? In order to solve these difficult points, even though we say that we are depending on the client's self-healing power, we have to recognize that the client now needs a psychotherapist.

The work of psychotherapists varies a great deal, depending on the case. Jung classified the work of psychotherapy in four categories: confession, elucidation, education, and transformation. The fourth is the most characteristic of Jung's focus. In this work of transformation, Jung said, "The therapist is no longer the agent of treatment but a fellow participant in a process of individual development."[1] Jung also stated, "No longer is he [the therapist] the superior wise man, judge, and counselor; he is a fellow participant who finds himself involved in the dialectical process just as deeply as the so-called patient."[2] In short, Jung pointed out clearly how important the relationship between patient and therapist is and the way such a relation is different from the general conception of "healer" and the person "healed." It is impressive that Jung clarified this point some time ago.

I basically agree with Jung's ideas, and I have made a great effort to actualize such a mode of practice. I would like to relate the above to Buddhism. By way of introduction, I shall describe my experience.

1. *Igyo* [Easy Doing]

Carl Jung's words quoted above were written in the early part of 1930. It is surprising to realize that he had recognized the essence of human relations in psychotherapy that early. About 1950, when I started counseling in Japan, such a practice was unheard of. At that time, the most influential theories on Japanese counseling and psychotherapy were those of the American clinical psychologist Carl A. Rogers. I too had read his books eagerly. So when I returned from my studies in Zurich, I felt that it would be quite a challenge to communicate Jung's thought to Japanese Rogerians, who were spread all over Japan.

I suppose that Rogers was influential in Japan to such an extent especially because, as he was understood there, he emphasized practice over theory. His way of working quickly got connected to *kata* [form] and *igyo* [easy doing], which are important concepts in the Japanese art world.[3] Therefore his style was easily accepted by the Japanese. Of course, such Japanese understanding in fact differed from Rogers' ideas, as there was the Buddhistic world view in the background. When you recall those ideas discussed in chapter 3, you will begin to understand this point.

When you learn art forms, individual uniqueness is not

required; everybody at the starting line is thought to be equal. But in order to become a good artist, you need to embody or master a certain appropriate "form" [kata]. Anyone who embodies the kata becomes a good artist. That's called igyo, i.e., "easy to do." If you have seen or participated in the tea ceremony, for example, you have an idea of what I mean. The actions in the tea room are prescribed in detail; after repeating the same actions many times, a person "embodies" the form. Then, without any question about the person's uniqueness or talent, he or she will become a "tea master." Here, igyo means that anyone can achieve mastery; but, in order to achieve such a goal, it is considered necessary to struggle hard before one can possibly embody the kata. We cannot forget this point.

Of course I need to add that this is not the only thing the Japanese art world is built on. In order to become a true master, it is necessary ultimately to have yurameki [literally, swaying back and forth], which "breaks" such a kata. After the mastery of strict kata, one's own yurameki results in a very slight shift, and one looks for and appreciates the beauty in that difference from the basic kata.

At the starting line, everyone is equal, and one's uniqueness or talent is not discussed. To become art which will be appreciated as Art, it must be expressed in kata form. At the root of this view lies the attitude of the Arising of True Nature, which, according to Hua-yen thought, means there is no self-nature, but the emptied Principle will self-divide into all the separate things. To embody such a kata, it is necessary to practice hard and long. But then, pushing beyond this, at the point of yurameki, breaking the kata, the uniqueness of the person will manifest itself for the first time. Achieving this is most difficult; therefore, most people will concentrate only on the igyo, mastery of a kata.

When I started my psychotherapy practice, Rogerian theory was being presented as "nondirective counseling." It was accepted as being well-suited to the Japanese psychological nature. Anyone will become a good counselor if he or she embodies the *kata* of "nondirective." But, in order to master that *kata* of "nondirective," the students had to receive very strict direction from their teachers, with much blood and tears.

As Rogers developed his ideas further, the Japanese followed. I think his basic attitude in psychotherapy was not too different from what Jung presented, and I have quoted some relevant passages above. Jung thought that, in order to become an analyst, it was necessary to be analyzed, in order to obtain the basic attitude for the therapy. He also pointed out that, in some cases, the therapist's role would change. This point is not made in Rogers' work. Consequently, the Japanese, even though following the development of Rogers' ideas, kept the *igyo* approach. In the United States, people who have the modern ego practice Rogers' ideas easily without loss of identity. In contrast, to embody the *kata* as *igyo* in Japan, effort was expended to negate ego. Working in this way, some degree of success was achieved in therapy, but there were times when the therapy did not go as well as expected.

I followed this Japanese tendency in my initial counseling work, but, probably because I was more attracted to the Western ego, I felt that something was not right. My gut feeling was: "If I keep doing this, my clients may get well, but I will be dead." Unless one has theories one can rely on and also understands how and why the client gets better, it's no good. So, I thought, to develop good theories and understanding, I would have to study in the United States. As mentioned above, doing so led me to study Jungian psychology.

2. Level of Relationship
Previously I remarked that the heaviest impact I experienced while studying at the C. G. Jung Institute in Zurich came from Western consciousness. I was trained to develop a strong Western ego; but, of course, this did not mean that I was able to develop the same ego as Westerners. And, on the other

hand, I paid a lot of attention to the importance of Self, recognizing that ego is not the primary focus.

As soon as I returned to Japan, I began to practice psychotherapy. There I was the only Jungian analyst for some time. But, fortunately, I was able to advance psychotherapy itself, as well as to disseminate Jungian psychotherapy widely.

As I began my practice, I was impressed by how strong the Mother archetype was. In the background of every interpersonal relationship, there was the powerful functioning of the Mother archetype. There was no exception to this in the client-therapist relationship.

The dominance of the Mother archetype, especially in regard to Buddhism, manifested itself beautifully in the well-known dream of Shinran Shonin (1173–1262), who developed the new *Shin* [Truth] sect of Pure Land Buddhism, which even today has numerous devotees. In Buddhism, there has always been a strict rule prohibiting monks from having intimate relations with women. In Japan, however, this prohibition was consistently broken. "He who hides it is a sage; he who abstains is a Buddha," was an old quotation. In Shinran's time, someone had written, "Nowadays, the sages who hide it are few; the Buddha who abstains is rarer still." Such was the state of things at that time. In such a state, Shinran, seemingly alone, suffered from the dilemma that, while he should be keeping the religious precepts, he could not control his desire for women. When he was about thirty years old, tormented by his own sexual urges, he undertook a one-hundred-day retreat to get dream oracles to resolve his dilemma.[4] At dawn on the ninety-fifth day, he had a dream in which the figure of Kannon, the Bodhisattva of Compassion, who was enshrined in that temple, appeared and spoke to him:

> When the devotee finds himself bound, through the working out of his past karma, to come into [sexual] contact with the female sex, I will incarnate myself as a beautiful

woman and become the object of his love. Throughout his life, I will be his helpmate for the sake of embellishing this world: and on his deathbed, I will lead him to Amida's Land of Bliss.

Through these words the Bodhisattva Kannon declared his Vow. He designated that I should make this known to all.

In this dream, the Bodhisattva said to Shinran, suffering so from the conflict between his monastic vow of celibacy and his need to express his sexual nature, that He, Kannon, would become woman, to fulfill Shinran's desires, and He would guide the devotee to Paradise at the time of death. Here is the Mother archetype, clear and simple. In general, Japanese clients project such a Bodhisattva figure onto the therapist. And the therapists also, consciously or not, try to play the Bodhisattva role.

Here, the Mother archetype is a positive one; but, of course, this principle certainly has its negative aspect as well. When Japanese people, consciously influenced by Euro-American culture, try to become independent, they soon realize the negative side of the Mother archetype. I have often witnessed images in analysands' dreams clearly reflecting the negative Mother archetype.

In this way, I found the function of the Mother archetype, whether positive or negative, in every human relationship. It became evident to me that separating the images into those of the personal level and those of the archetypal level helped a great deal to clarify the client's problems and to understand the nature of our therapist-client relationship. But, as I've mentioned many times, the difficulty I encountered here was that, due to the characteristics of the Japanese ego, it is very difficult to objectify psychic phenomena and to verbalize such experience.

Before discussing that problem further, I will comment on the manner of relating at the preverbal level. To verbalize the relationship with the client, the therapist must objectify it. But to a Japanese client, that sounds like the relationship itself is being cut. In contrast to a relationship between two Westerners, which exists between their two independent egos, the Japanese case can hardly be called "relationship," because of the oneness at the base of the togetherness. So it is difficult to make the client conscious of the condition of "relationship." Before verbalizing about the client's being surrounded by the Mother archetype, the therapist has been functioning as the archetypal Mother without being aware of it. Furthermore, if the therapist were to refuse to do so, the therapeutic relationship would be cut off.

In the early period, my practice was going well, but then gradually I started seeing truly difficult clients. I was affected more and more by these relationships per se. Suffering, I still worked very hard, though not grasping the core issue of relationship. Although I tried as a therapist to follow Jung's word—to be "a fellow participant in a process of individual development"[5]—I felt it as too destructive or as an unbearable burden. I still kept the way, but it seemed that suicide was highly probable. I realized that, if I continued this way, I would be in danger of death from exhaustion. It must have been hard indeed for those people around me who supported me during the time I was in such a state.

Then I started to notice that the level of relationship which the client was needing and the level of relationship which I as the therapist was putting so much effort into were different. While the movement happening in my client was toward the archetypal level, I somehow was trying to respond at the more superficial "personal" level. I was, for instance, trying to be a Bodhisattva with the superficial part of myself. It was impossible to satisfy my client, even though I fully intended to. While my client would appreciate my effort at the superficial level, at times when the path was not clear and the client was feeling deeply dissatisfied, the client would either verbalize her or his state, saying, "I want to die," or simply would take action, i.e., act out. The effect on me was that my superficial part would accelerate its effort or just give up, seeing things as hopeless.

Trying to understand what I had been doing in my own consciousness, I gradually comprehended these issues through Buddhist ideas like those presented in chapter 3. The Hua-yen teaching of Interdependent Origination suggested a profound dimension to the therapist-client relationship. Now, when I meet with a person, there is a vast expansion of the world, and I am floating in the evolving relationship. The relationship is quite "impersonal," in that it is quite different from our daily human relationship. I have tried to maintain this impersonal relationship, although it is quite difficult to do so. There are still some people who say they want to commit suicide or some who may act out. With this fresh approach, however, the numbers decreased. My exhaustion dissipated. I was able then to see more people who were thought to be truly difficult cases. Thinking back on all this, I can see how much effort I initially expended, yet it did not yield much fruit. My own maturation was needed.

Among those who value the importance of personal relationship, some may misunderstand this approach as affirming the neutrality of the psychotherapist, so I would like to clarify this a little more. When you gain an attitude such as I have been describing, frequently you can become much more open to express your full range of feelings: sadness, anger, joy, or sorrow. When you try to accept the client's deep inner psychic content with only your shallow level of consciousness, your personal feelings probably will seem repressed. But after expanding into a deep, "impersonal" relationship, your personal feelings become free. In short, the level of relationship shifts as is needed.

Basically, I tend to inhibit any expression of my anger, but recently I have been able to express my anger straightforwardly toward clients. When we expose emotion, obviously ego is engaged, but the root of it is often deep in the impersonal layer; therefore, to express such emotion seems to me significant in terms of deepening a given human relationship. Anyway, I have been less likely to take it out on my acquaintances or family—i.e., "dump" a distorted emotion which was suppressed during a therapy session. Also, my fatigue does not accumulate any longer.

3. The Awakening of Faith

After developing such therapeutic relationships, my work became much easier. But, practicing in this way, I still recognized that there were innate conflicts, or perhaps I should call it a certain splitting of consciousness. I have said that I have gained a lot from Buddhist teaching but also that I have not had the experience of my consciousness reaching down to the deepest level of existence. In the therapy session, however, my consciousness is able to experience simultaneously personal and impersonal levels, or a kind of wandering here and there. This is my actual condition. It is almost impossible to verbalize it. For example, a person says he wants to die immediately. Then my consciousness experiences simultaneously: "Absolutely No!" and "Un-hunh, I understand your feeling," and "Go ahead, if you say so." It is impossible to integrate these. But then I have learned through such experiences that the most effective way to resolve this "conflict" is to maintain the posture of waiting, holding all the conflicting elements as long as possible.

Just recently, I learned how to explain such a practice of psychotherapy, while exploring the inspirational sutra called *The Awakening of Faith in the Mahayana* [Sanskrit.: *Mahayana-sraddhotpada-sastra*; Chinese: *Ta-ch'eng ch'i-hsin lun*; Japanese: *Daijo-kishiron*[6]]. I learned about the sutra through Dr. Toshihiko Izutsu's book, *Philosophy of the Awakening of the Faith in the Mahayana.*[7] I am sorry to say that this was Dr. Izutsu's final work. But I am grateful that I can discuss this late sutra according to his interpretation. Although this Awakening of Faith sutra is attributed to Asvaghosha, its actual writer is unknown. Yet it has been a great force for change in the history of Far Eastern Buddhism from the sixth century to the present.

The two notable characteristics of this work are: (1) the spatial structure of its ideas, and (2) the manner in which the ideas develop—that is, in a double form, or through conflicting aspects. First of all, the text, in dealing with the psyche or consciousness, conceptualizes its ideas in a spatial and territorial manner. Actually, Freud and Jung also have done this in their depth psychology. Therefore, it is the second characteristic that we need to focus on. I was attracted to this work because it involves containing contradictions just as they come and not taking the direction of integrating them for resolution. The logical development of the argument proceeds in a delicate, nonlinear, snake-like, swaying movement, maintaining the double aspect of two conflicting ways. Izutsu says that, if we try to read the text in one direction, as if it were stretched into a straight line, the idea of the *Awakening of the Faith* may appear to be full of internal contradictions.

The text intertwines ontology and the theory of consciousness so closely as to make them inseparable. At first, it speaks about ontology. But soon one realizes that, at the same time, it is giving a description of consciousness.

The key term in this text is *tathagata-garbha* [Absolute-embryo, Absolute-receptacle], usually translated as *Suchness*. Suchness is the totality of the nondividing, indivisible, generating power of being. It is the life force that fills the infinite cosmos and yet in essence is absolute Nothingness and Emptiness. But, at the same time, Suchness is "Being," or "phenomenal self-manifestation." Suchness consists of two aspects. One is the Suchness of all things in their totality of nondiscrimination, which transcends all forms of verbalization or conceptualization; this is called "Suchness separated from words." The other is when all things are infinitely differentiated; this is called "Suchness relying on words." But we cannot forget to see these two aspects in their totality, which is Suchness.

In *The Awakening of Faith* sutra, the term *Suchness* is used to mean the Mind. In other words, the Suchness without verbalization is absolute, undifferentiated, nonphenomenal consciousness. This is consciousness of Nothingness, but it is wrong to understand this as passive and negative. Because it is "empty" consciousness, it has the endless possibility of phenomenal, "non-empty" consciousness.

Contrary to this, Suchness dependent on verbalization is the consciousness which is working toward the phenomenal world's divided dimension, and we should say that this is what we ordinarily consider to be the realm of consciousness. However, this involves a certain part, the so-called "unconscious." The reason I say "the so-called 'unconscious'" is that, in depth psychology, the viewpoint is based only on the ego side. Naturally, the remainder of its own realm outside itself will, as a whole, be called "the unconscious." Above I commented that in, Buddhism, this "unconscious" is merely considered to be the consciousness of different levels. Therefore it is hard to discuss these views in a completely parallel manner. When you see that, in the structure of the psyche according to *The Awakening of Faith,* ego has no determined place, you can understand.

DIAGRAM:

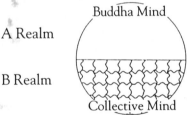

A Realm   Buddha Mind   Mind Suchness (Absolute)

B Realm   Collective Mind   Mind Birth-Death (Phenomenal)

Using the diagram of Dr. Izutsu, I will try to clarify this. Here you see the divided realm, A and B. The diagram is presenting both Mind and ontology. It consists of a divided consciousness: A, the undivided state of no verbalization; and B, the innumerable existences principle. Here this diagram is also used for the Mind as it is. Realm A is called Mind-Suchness (Absolute), which is Emptiness consciousness; and realm B is the fully divided phenomenal consciousness, called Mind–Birth/Death (Phenomenal). When this Mind-Suchness has religious significance, it is called "Buddha Mind."

Realm B needs explanation, because it differs from the Western assumption that ego equals consciousness. "Consciousness" here does not mean personal consciousness but focuses on the transpersonal nature of consciousness. Dr. Izutsu suggests thinking of Jung's Collective Unconscious as the *consciousness* of such a Collective Unconscious. Jung chose that name because he was viewing it from the ego's perspective. If, in contrast, we start from the complete nondivision of Mind-Suchness, we would then consider the Collective Unconscious also as conscious but at an extremely deep level where it is transpersonal, expanding to the whole of humankind. This way of thinking is close to Jung's idea.

This sort of transpersonal, total-consciousness field in *The Awakening of Faith* sutra is called "Shujo-shin," or "Collective Mind." This Collective Mind has two aspects. It has the expansion of cognitive total-unity, which contains every kind of existence, including Jung's Collective Unconscious. At the same time, it has our ordinary daily consciousness. That is, it is constantly swinging back and forth between ordinary consciousness and the transpersonal, cosmic cognition. *The Awakening of Faith* states that this Collective Mind totally embraces daily phenomena and the superexperiential, metaphysical world.

This seemingly contradictory nature of Collective Mind is related to how you view this phenomenal world, or "Reality," in Western terms. That is, the world of the phenomenal is only the world of delusion, insofar as you take the world of Mind-Suchness to be important. If we are not careful, modern man may be possessed by the world of delusion into which we have put so much unnecessary effort. It is hard for us to agree that everything is delusion. Actually this phenomenal world is the manifestation of Suchness. *The Awakening of Faith* tells us that, even though it appears to be changing ceaselessly, the essential aspect of Buddha mind is not damaged or spoiled. Therefore Collective Mind is united, paradoxically, with Buddha Mind.

As you read this sutra, you tend to swing one way and then the other, and you wonder which way is right. This sort of experience corresponds to my clinical experience with patients. The person who teaches Buddhist doctrine emphasizes the wonder of Buddha Mind too heavily and then strongly attacks the delusions of the phenomenal world, which appears to be opposed to Buddha Mind. Quite simply, it sounds like: "If you put out a lot of effort to 'empty the ego,' you will know the existence of 'True Suchness.'" Probably such a stance is due to a narrow understanding of Buddhism. Dr. Mokusen Miyuki, a Jungian analyst and Buddhist priest, also points to such misunderstanding. My attitude as a psychotherapist is to relate to both the superficial and the deep layers of consciousness at the same time, and to pay attention to the details of external reality but simultaneously place no special importance on any of it. I feel that such a paradoxical attitude is supported by *The Awakening of Faith in the Mahayana*.

4. Alaya-Vijnana

The relationship between Mind-Suchness (A area) and Mind–Birth/Death (B area) is subtle indeed, and it is obvious that they are not clearly distinguishable. B is simply A's self-divided form. A is basically transposable to B through its tendency toward phenomena, and again B has the tendency to return to the original A.

In this particular text, this mutual transformation field of A and B is called *alaya-vijnana*. While this is an important term in classical Buddhist thought, we need to recognize that it is used with a different meaning here.

Alaya-vijnana is a flexible compound which encompasses both these areas of Mind (A and B). The text describes it as "the harmonious unity of Non-being-destruction and Being-destruction; not one but not different." So the *alaya-vijnana* has two aspects: (1) its function of "awareness," moving in the A direction; and (2) its function of "no-awareness," moving in the B direction. If the *alaya-vijnana* is forgetting the A direction or not noticing it, just concentrating on ordinary phenomena, this would be "no-awareness." The text has a detailed description of the process of falling into the direction of "no-awareness." As I was reading that passage, I just burst into laughter, because it sounded like the process of "no-awareness" was so similar to the Western process of "ego-formation"!

Another thing I noticed was that, finally, here in *The Awakening of Faith*, the individual becomes related. The function of *alaya-vijnana* relates to both aspects A and B, so how to "unify" these aspects depends on the individual way of handling it. In Western depth psychology, development theoretically starts from the individual ego and, in the case of Jung, leads down to the layer of the Collective Unconscious. In this sutra text, the transpersonal and no-division world is presented first, and then, finally, the individual is discreetly discussed. Thinking in this way, Eastern and Western ideas are, at a glance, not too different from each other.

According to this treatise, the *alaya-vijnana* moves toward A, the way to "awareness." But this move by itself does not achieve full awareness. After reaching the outermost bounds, it turns back toward B and ultimately reaches the state of viewing both realms A and B nondiscriminatingly and with wholeness, which is itself "awareness." We also can know that reaching to the bounds of A means at the same time reaching the edges of B, being aware of the truth of B. When such a state of consciousness is realized in an existential way, it is "awareness." But clearly, reaching the limits of A is almost impossible for us ordinary people. We tend to wander in the realm of no-awareness only. I like these descriptions of *The Awakening of Faith*. I accept its teaching in my own peculiar way. When asked, "Why do you do such an arbitrary thing?," I have to answer simply, "Because I am a psychotherapist, not a theologian nor a religious teacher."

Among all the various ideas of Buddhism, one never

comes across the kingdom of the modern Western ego—at the end of the *alaya-vijnana's* swing in the B direction, for example. Though I acknowledge its value and strength, I do not think that the ego which emerged in the West is the final answer. Japan, an Eastern country, has benefited from the numerous blessings created by Western ego. We cannot forget about this reality.

Some people practice very hard on the A direction and, upon reaching its limit, swing back toward B. But, due to their concentration upon "non-ego," when they are exposed to the temptations of life as lived from a Western ego perspective, they often have lost the ability to discern correctly. Even while they think they have gained *satori*, they are drowning in our age's abundance of material delusions and goods. I hope many of us don't make this mistake.

So, what I thought at this point is that, as ordinary people, even when we are putting lots of effort into swinging toward B, we must be aware of its "non-awareness" and not forget the necessity of swinging back in the A direction. Speaking more positively, if one reaches the limit of A and turns back toward B, it is possible to unify A and B. Then, moving in the B direction though not reaching the limit yet, I could say that a step toward B means a step toward A, depending on one's awareness. Again, one could say, though expending great effort in the B direction, do not place priority on that.

Do you remember the case of the woman to whom I told the story "Drawn by a Cow; Worshipping at Zenkoji"? She came first to talk about her daughter-in-law and then gradually became interested in the religious world. She read religious books and went to hear famous religious teachers. Yet she could not settle her mind. Then she had the following dream.

> A famous priest came to our neighborhood to give a sermon. Hearing the news, I rushed to the place, but the sermon was already finished. As I was going back with great disappointment, the priest appeared and said, "I will teach you a

specially important thing." I was overjoyed. Then he handed me a *zokin* [a thick, stitched rag for polishing floors]. I woke up, flabbergasted.

This dream seemed to her nonsense, rather than merely strange. While we talked about it, she recognized that actually it was more important for her to polish with a rag than listen to another sermon. Having a housekeeper at that time, she did not need to do such work, but she started to polish the hallway with a *zokin*. It seemed to me that this work swung both in the B direction and in the A direction. Another impressive thing is that the great priest in the dream gave her "individual" instruction rather than a public sermon. This was something meaningful just to her. So the dreamer felt actualized. This example taught me that it is possible to move in both A and B directions, even though not reaching the limit of one of them first. Because of this, she doesn't recommend that others practice her floor-polishing, nor do I. This way of unifying movements toward A and B is, I think, quite individualized.

5. Symptoms and Koans

In regard to Zen, I have no experience of *sanzen* (interviews with a Zen master), nor have I read many books on the subject. But I have had many occasions to listen to stories of friends and acquaintances who have had such experience. These have been stories of direct experiences, and I received responses to my uninhibited questions, so I have learned a lot. And I have felt that my work as a psychotherapist is somewhat similar to Zen.

Zen in Japan has the *Soto* and *Rinzai* schools. Both focus on *zazen* [Zen meditation], although Soto stresses "just sitting," while *Rinzai* favors interviews and koans given by a mature teacher. When I sit with a client in the therapy session, I am sometimes reminded of the motto, "Just sitting," appreciated by the *Soto* monks—not caught by "treatment" or "solution," but simply sitting. I sometimes feel that way. I mean that such times have simply happened, although I was not, and am not, aiming for them. According to the client's situation, we may talk about daily life. But sometimes it happens to be close to the situation of "just sitting." This seems appropriate.

Speaking of koans, sometimes I feel that clients' complaints are similar to koans, at least for the therapist. One of the famous koans is: "Bringing both hands together quickly produces a clap. What is the sound with one hand?" It is obvious to anyone that you don't get the answer by rational thinking. It seems as though a koan is given to create an opportunity to allow the whole person to relate to deeper consciousness, instead of relying on the superficial consciousness. Let's think about this, using the example of a symptom that a client complains about. It is not possible to resolve this by rational thinking. Then the therapist asks for the client's free associations or for the client to focus on dreams. This means giving up looking for resolution from superficial consciousness and searching for the answer from one's depths. Both koan and symptom function similarly here.

However, in some mild case of hysteria, the client's complex or conflict in the unconscious becomes readily conscious and thus comes to resolution. If we look at this according to the koan and Buddhist ideas, the client was given the koan (the symptom) and abandoned it in the middle, not reaching the depths of the psyche but turning back to the other direction, helped by the therapist. That is to say, the therapist's effort actually took away the rare opportunity for a *satori* experience.

I like to think this way at times: when the client suffers a symptom, it's meaningful to resolve it—but also not to resolve it. It all depends on following the person's process of individuation. I cannot help but become very cautious in a psychotherapy session. Of course, the conscious appeal at the beginning is to resolve the symptom quickly, so we cannot forget about that. But I am facing the total being of the client and need to be cautious. My attitude needs to be flexible.

Otherwise, I don't see the way the individuation process wants to go. One's consciousness has to be as mobile as possible in order to move freely between the surface and the depths. Then one can see the direction to go with the client.

So-called "borderline" patients have a stronger tendency, compared with others, I think, to move toward the A realm and neglect the B realm. So, in their treatment, tasks are accomplished in the B realm—for example, structuring daily life, becoming able to hold a part-time job, etc. On such occasions, if the therapist gets excited or even pleased with the progress, these people may take it as the therapist's neglect or rejection of the importance of work in the A realm. Then they might become angry with the unsuspecting therapist and even act it out. In this sort of event, I see the similarity to a koan. You work very hard and think you have the real answer; but, just then the master strikes you with his stick, shouting, "Katsu!" Of course I have to say that our masters—that is, our clients—do not themselves know the answer and so are different from Zen masters. Yet we also must realize that, even though they don't know the right answer beforehand, they can clearly discern whether what we do is appropriate or not.

While I have no experience of sitting *zazen*, I think I have been trained a great deal by my excellent teachers. I am most grateful to them. I am still pleased when a symptom is resolved. But, since I was well-trained by them, basically I now have the attitude cultivated by the above experiences: good if alleviated, good as well if not alleviated. Even if one koan is solved, the next one will come. So, actually, we have an infinite number of koans around our respective environments.

But if I think of the deeply subtle union of the A and the B realms, just being caught in the A realm only and not able to do anything in daily life is not admirable. Whenever extreme apathy has overwhelmed Japanese youth, I have thought that they received the koan of moving toward the A direction. But, not aware of it at all, they felt that doing things in the B realm was totally worthless, so they fell into the state of doing nothing. Rather than teaching such apathetic youth the meaning of work or the value of social activity, I met with them to find the koan together. This search often takes a long time, but I still feel that my attitude toward these clients is appropriate.

6. Interpretation and Language

In psychotherapy, language has a primary role to play. It's almost all done through language. In Jungian practice, images in dreams, paintings, sandplay, and clay work are very important. But dreams are reported by words. The interpretation of images is expressed by language. Contrary to this, Buddhism, it seems to me, has a basic tendency not to rely on, or even positively to mistrust, language. I have remarked many times that Absolute Being is considered "preverbal," as indicated in the expression "Suchness without words."

Shizuteru Ueda, a scholar of religion who also has Zen experience, says, "Zen seems to dislike words excessively." Indeed, "Without words" is a Zen motto. But Ueda points out in his next sentence: "On the other hand, Zen has given birth to numerous words."[8] When you go to any bookstore, you will find many books on Zen. So how can you call this "without words"? The Zen enlightenment itself probably is impossible to verbalize. If you try, even a million words may not suffice. Though we have many books, our basic attitude is that, without an essential experience, uttering many words is useless.

In contrast, the psychotherapy that developed in the West considers language important. For instance, chased by a lion in a dream, you run away with all your might. Even though you have "experienced" this, it seems necessary to verbalize the interpretation of its meaning. By the way, what does *meaning* mean here? There is meaning when the content of the dream is well-connected to the dreamer's consciousness system. When this does not happen, the dream, in the Western sense, has no meaning.

If one inquires about the meaning of a person's dream, various responses may come: I dreamed this because I saw a movie before I went to bed in which the main character was chased by a lion, or the lion represents my father and I must run from him in fear, or I'm glad I was not eaten up, or in such an encounter I should have challenged the lion and not run away, etc. There are many possible ways to find meanings, and it is not so much a problem of which is "correct." What was discovered and what was gained for one's way of life from such interpretation—these seem important.

In accord with our discussion above concerning the function of the *alaya-vijnana*, a dream bifurcates. On the one hand, it moves as descriptive words toward Mind—Birth/ Death (B realm) and yields meanings. On the other hand, if you work it in the Mind-Suchness direction (A realm), it will manifest the Mind which is no other expression than "!" and which reflects the pre-division state of the dream. When from out of Mind-Suchness, the "!" experience is manifested and divided as the dream of a lion, then the interpretation will lose words.

Jung seemed to recognize this when he distinguished symbol and sign. The content of a symbol is not easily replaceable by content one already knows. Its manifestation is its most appropriate expression. There is no way to replace it. I think his emphasis on this point indicates his style of dream interpretation. He disliked for anyone to forget this point and just interpret dreams according to ready-made theories or known ideas. His warning, "Do anything you like, only don't try to understand [dreams],"[9] reflects his attitude well.

With this in mind, one can respond to dreams in an understanding direction and a nonunderstanding direction. Jung, of course, takes the latter as more important. If we transpose this stance into the Buddhist *alaya-vijnana* mode, we might say that its functioning in the Mind–Birth/Death is the understanding dream direction, while its functioning in Mind-Suchness is the nonunderstanding dream direction.

Of course, we know that Jung has expressed himself in his unique paradoxical way, as already mentioned. If we take the attitude that the Western "ego" is important, then the

Eastern "True Suchness" is also important. Accordingly, we would also appreciate the importance of both understanding a dream and nonunderstanding a dream. Or we might spend our entire effort on interpretation, while also remembering nevertheless that that is not the primary importance of the dream. Amplification, which Jung established regarding dream content, is an effective method. Similarly, using the contents of amplification also has two directions, understanding and nonunderstanding. We cannot forget that both are important. Then, to push a bit further, by the amplification of nonunderstanding, we open ourselves to discovery.

A certain client of mine lamented, "I can't understand dreams as easily as your book does." I explained to her that I think both the understandable and the not understandable ones are important; but, in a book, you can present only the understandable ones. In order to experience a not understandable one, you must deliberately meet an analyst.

Perhaps because I am Japanese, I have the tendency to value not understanding as slightly more important than understanding. In the above, I have used the terms "Western ego" and "Eastern True Suchness" to avoid using the words "ego" and "Self," so very familiar to Jungians; even though I think of Self as important, I did not want you to think simply in terms of "understanding" dreams along the ego-Self axis.

When "True Suchness without words" becomes most important, we psychotherapists can only keep silent. But if, after listening to the client's dream, you simply remain silent, the relationship will probably be cut. So eventually I will talk. There are times, however, when I imagine being in the *Garland Sutra*. The central figure, Vairocana, speaks no word. The surrounding Bodhisattvas are giving sermons assumed to be expressing the Thought of Vairocana. Then, in the psychotherapy session, I wonder if, with Vairocana in the center, we may presume to speak his words. That is to say, the center is the silence. . . . Words are there, our words, as its manifestation.

Now, to verbalize is to objectify phenomena. When a Japanese client accepts the therapeutic relation as establishing fundamental oneness with the therapist, it is problematical. That is why in Japan, as noted above, if the relationship is objectified clearly, the client takes this as actually breaking the relationship. For this reason, it is important to have verbal expression with silence placed in the center.

The Japanese language itself quite simply reflects this way of thinking. It is possible, for example, to have a form of speech that does not differentiate between subject and object. By using such a mode of expression, one can resolve to a certain extent this problem of verbalization breaking the relationship. In conversation, we often keep subject or object rather vague and still maintain "communication." Obviously I have to omit actual Japanese examples, but to give you an explanation would involve a longer discourse. I will try to express it with an image. It is not therapist facing client, thrusting interpretations at her or him. Rather, the two are sitting together, facing the same direction and, trying to be mindful of the Vairocana's intention, uttering some words. Perhaps this is close to it.

7. Gentle Sorrow

When our human relations expand beyond the personal level into the impersonal realm, the experience which is flowing at its deepest level can hardly be called a feeling; maybe "sorrow" is suitable. The ancient Japanese word *kanashi* [sadness or melancholy] includes *itoshii*, meaning "loving" or "tender feeling." I should say it does have such a mixture of feelings.

I have seen such a delicate, yet strongly felt, experience expressed in a sandplay scene. It was made by a woman in her thirties. The most impressive feature in the scene was an additional sandplay scene made within a larger whole one. In the small box were parents and a child, house, trees, and a cat—an ordinary scene. At the back of the larger box rose a mountain enveloped in mist, and I noticed a snake peeking out of a cave on the mountain and glass beads falling down the mountainside. The client said they were tears. In the front part was a river with fish swimming in it, all in one direction. And she said she could not explain why she made this.

When I saw this sandplay, I recalled the Buddhist world view that we have been considering here. That is, I felt that the world in the small scene represented our daily phenomenal world and that, surrounding it, was enormous energy flowing out, as shown by the snake and flowing river. What in this scene made the strongest impact on me was the tears. Whose tears was not the question, for they were somewhat impersonal, crystallizing the deep-flowing and sorrowful feelings of the larger scene, by which daily life is supported. The smaller box indicates what may be joyous and cheerful, but that world is supported by the deep melancholic feeling which cannot quite be called "sorrow."

There is another sandplay image which indicates this feeling in a bit different form. This is from my first sandplay case, so it has been unforgettable. It was made by a nineteen-year-old young man, whom I mentioned before in connection with the Bodhisattva dream. He suffered social phobia, blushing repeatedly; due to this he stayed at home. After a long treatment, he regained his vitality and was able to go to college, although occasionally he stayed home out of anxiety and suffering. At that time, I was working very hard to cure my patients, so I kept encouraging him not to be defeated by his reality. That's when he made this scene.

In the center, he buried a boy in sand, leaving his face exposed. Then he placed fire around him, with terrible-looking monsters surrounding it. Here I felt that his anxiety and suffering were transmitted to me just as they were. The boy buried in the sand seemed to be weeping. Behind those monsters were flower beds and women in what appeared to be a joyful scene. But the two parts looked so isolated from each other that "reconciliation" seemed impossible. And then the client placed two people in the front area. Without explanation, I understood they indicated therapist and client. After finishing this, he said, "I tried to show how terrible my suffering is at present. Then, while I was placing these figures, part of myself was already gradually approaching a quite joyous world, led by my therapist's guidance." I was so happy that I told him, "Together, we will put our effort into going toward such a pleasant world." My attention rushed in the joyful direction.

Luckily, this patient did get better, and I happily presented slides of his sandplay at some conferences, as he had made ten more interesting scenes. In this key scene, I thought that the figure at the center was the client suffering from the symptom, who then, with the therapist's help, was able to find his healthy part. I was assuming that the role of the therapist was just like that of the figure placed together with another at the front. But then, while I was explaining this case, I got some different ideas regarding what he had said.

If you compare this sandplay with the sandplay discussed just before this one, you will find the similarity. I now began to see that the pleasant world he placed outside was supported by the suffering and sorrow of the center. And the reason only one person was placed at the center is this: it is the world which comes before division of subject-object, and this is logically represented by one person. Then, when coming closer to the daily level, the division occurs. This was appropriately represented by the two figures, therapist and client. My misunderstanding of the therapist's role actually created more suffering for the client and prolonged the treatment.

I believe the primary role of a therapist is to situate oneself at the center, while being inseparable from the client at the deepest level of suffering and sorrow. Then, naturally, the daily world starts to open up, and there both are able to experience a lot of pleasant and cheerful things. Even though I stress sorrow, I am not leading my life every day depressed and full of tears. Rather, I would say that I have come to enjoy cheerful occasions more often. Instead of teaching the client how good such a cheerful world is, I try to situate myself in the sorrowful center when I do psychotherapy. When you are there for some time, the enjoyable world naturally opens up.

8. A Science of Human Beings

Earlier I talked about ancient Buddhist stories. Now, at the conclusion of these lectures, I would like to consider the possibility that what I have discussed may contribute to the development of a "new science." As I have mentioned, modern science is quite effective for manipulating things, for mechanisms, but it is not suited to grasp living things as a whole. So I think it is necessary to have a new science, in order to comprehend the human being as a whole. But the premise would be the existence of an investigator-phenomena relationship, differing from the methodology of modern science. While exploring how such a relationship might function, it would try to include the phenomena experienced by the different levels of consciousness and not simply by the consciousness now being applied to the study of modern science.

When you look at the relationships between things from the standpoint of the idea in Buddhism called *pratitya-samutpada* [*engi* in Japanese], the dynamic, simultaneous, and interdependent emergence and existence of all things becomes significant. That is to say, one attends not only to causal relationships, but also to synchronistic or acausal relationships. And the knowledge you acquire there necessitates some sort of investigator's experience. This point is different from modern science, in which "universal" knowledge will be acquired without any direct relation to each individual experience.

The above matters are, I think, necessary as long as you are studying the "human being" as a whole. Despite being different from modern science, I still would call it "science," because it does not use the "Absolute," or dogma, to explain phenomena. It is based upon human experiences, and it looks for principles and constructs theories which are not absolute. It will treat such matters as dispensable and accordingly reflect experiential facts. Because of this quality, I think I can call this a science. But, unless we are well aware of the fact that this science is different from modern science, the result easily could become associated with magic.

I cannot knowledgeably contrast contemporary physics with classical physics, but I do know that today it is considered impossible to do research without taking into account the relationship between the observer and the phenomena observed. I am proposing my thoughts as a "science of the human being." I have a premonition that such a new science, covering the whole without making distinctions between things and human beings, will emerge, and that it will be infinitely closer to religion than the old (modern) science. At such a time, ideas from Buddhism, such as those of Hua-yen, will become useful.

As I close, I would like to relate my thoughts to a recent research report in the field of immunology. According to the research, three key bodily systems—the neurological system, the endocrine system, and the immune system—function independently yet work harmoniously together. There is no central system which integrates these three systems. Each of these functions within its own integration, and, in addition, they function well as a whole though not integrated by a central control. A friend of mine, Dr. Tomio Tada, declares, "The human body is a supersystem."[10]

Taking a hint from the above, I think that the human psyche also should be seen as a "supersystem." I have repeatedly discussed different levels of consciousness while also indicating that even logically conflicting things will coexist in the mind of a human being. Indeed, that coexistence has value. I am inclined to think that our human mind maintains integration in each of the different levels of consciousness. In addition, as a whole it functions as a supersystem without a center. In short, I think that the psyche as a whole, when it is healthy and functioning well, does not need to have an integrative center.

Carl Jung called the center of ordinary consciousness "ego," and, while the modern West thought of the ego as most important, Jung pointed out the significance of the Self. That is his great contribution. But we cannot forget the fact that Jung has given the Self an extremely paradoxical nature. He said that the Self is "the Center" and yet also emphasized its being "the Whole." I like the following anecdote. Jung was asked by his audience, "What is the Self? Please give us an example." His response was: "All of you!" They are not easily integrated.[11]

Some might say that, if a system as a whole is functioning well, you call it "integration." For integration, we tend to think that a principle or rule exists which should be central and controlling. I think that things—including human beings—work well beyond the center or principle which man creates.

I began this lecture series by talking about my personal experiences. I described my great trouble being caught between Eastern and Western cultures. While in such suffering, I believed in the integration of the two and talked about it easily. But, after trying hard many times, I gradually came to know that it is, in fact, impossible to "integrate" them. It even seems dangerous to attempt quick integration, as I have realized that people who attempt it tend to ignore things which are "inconvenient." So it seems likely that a new science would not try to develop a system of knowledge featuring simple, logical integration.

This explanation of integration versus nonintegration may, in the Western system of knowledge, seem confusing, even meaningless. Yet, if I can accept that conflict and contradiction are important; then, after determining that integration is impossible, I can add that, with time and insight, integration is also possible. This perhaps is not so threatening. If we are to develop this new science of the whole, we must open ourselves to imaginative ways of thinking and perceiving and summon up our most determined efforts.

Epilogue

C. G. Jung recounts an interesting episode in his "Psychology of the Transference":

> The enormous importance that Freud attached to the transference phenomenon became clear to me at our first personal meeting in 1907. After a conversation lasting many hours there came a pause. Suddenly he asked me out of the blue, "And what do you think about the transference?" I replied with the deepest conviction that it was the alpha and omega of the analytical method, whereupon he said, "Then you have grasped the main thing."[1]

Since then transference/countertransference has been one of the most important issues in the field of psychotherapy.

There is a story about two Zen monks which, for me, gives a hint of how to think about transference. Two monks are on a trip. On the way they have to cross a river on foot. Whereupon a beautiful lady comes there and seems to be reluctant to step into the river. A monk immediately embraces her and crosses the river. After that the two monks separate from her, and the monks go their way. The two walk for some time in silence. Suddenly one monk says to the other, "I have been kept thinking whether it is right or not that a Buddhist monk embrace a young woman, even though it is obviously helpful for her." The other answers: "Yes, I embraced her but left her when we crossed the river. You, on the other hand, have been embracing her until now."

There is a paradox in this story. The one who adhered to the precept of not touching women was obliged to retain erotic bondage to woman. The other monk, who was so free, reminds me of the image of winds, which touch, embrace, or sometimes beat persons and things yet never stay in one place.

For the consideration of transference/countertransference, it is sometimes helpful to take as models the relationships between parents and children, between lovers, siblings, or friends. But if you think only in that way, you tend to understand transference/countertransference as too much on a personal level and forget about soul. If you think of it taking as models the situation of individuals with stones, trees, rivers, winds, and other aspects of nature, the level of psychotherapy may become much deeper.

As David Rosen begins his foreword with a poem (haiku) by a famous Japanese author, I would like to close this epilogue with a poem by an unknown Western poet:

A THOUSAND WINDS

Do not stand at my grave and weep,
I am not there, I do not sleep.
I am a thousand winds that blow;
I am the diamond glints on snow.
I am the sunlight on ripened grain:
I am the gentle autumn's rain.

When you awake in the morning hush,
I am the swift uplifting rush
of quiet in circled flight.
I am the soft star that shines at night.

Do not stand at my grave and cry.
I am not there; I did not die.

—Author unknown[2]

Notes

Foreword

1. C. G. Jung, *Memories, Dreams, Reflections,* ed. Aniela Jaffe (New York: Pantheon, 1963), 20.

2. Thomas Merton, *The Asian Journal of Thomas Merton* (New York: New Directions, 1975), 104. During Thomas Merton's visit to the East, he discovered that Buddha encompassed both self and no-self; that is, he discovered "the Middle Way."

3. C. G. Jung, foreword to *Introduction to Zen Buddhism,* by Daisetsu T. Suzuki (New York: Doubleday, 1956), reprinted in *Psychology and Religion: East and West,* 2d ed., and in *The Collected Works of C. G. Jung,* ed. H. Read, M. Fordam, and G. Adler (Princeton, N.J.: Princeton Univ. Press, 1969), 11:538–39.

4. C. G. Jung, "On the Discourses of the Buddha," in *The Symbolic Life,* in *Collected Works of Jung* (1976), 18:693–99.

5. Jung, *The Symbolic Life,* in *Collected Works of Jung* (1976), 18:311.

Prologue

1. Erich Neumann, *The Origins and History of Con-*

sciousness (New York: Bollingen Foundation and Pantheon Books, 1954), 18.

2. Jung, "Foreword to *Introduction to Zen Buddhism*," in *Collected Works of Jung* (1958), 11:543.

3. Ibid., 11:554.

Chapter 1

1. For example, Dr. Mokusen Miyuki is both a Jungian analyst and a Buddhist priest. The book by J. Marvin Spiegelman and Mokusen Miyuki, *Buddhism and Jungian Psychology* (Phoenix, Ariz.: Falcon Press, l985), is quite revealing on this subject.

2. This point is discussed in the final chapter of Henri F. Ellenberger, *The Discovery of the Unconscious* (New York: Basic Books, 1970).

3. Ellenberger, *Discovery of the Unconscious*.

4. Hayao Kawai, "Genkei to shiteno Ro-nyaku Danjo" [Old, Young, Male, Female as Archetypes], in Kenzaburo Oe et al., eds. *Ro-nyaku no Jiku Danjo no Jiku* (Tokyo: Iwana sho-ten, 1982).

5. Eugen Herrigel, *Zen and the Art of Archery* (New York: Pantheon Books, 1953).

6. Jung, foreword to *Introduction to Zen Buddhism*, in *Collected Works of Jung* (1958), 11:538–57.

7. Neumann, *Origins and History of Consciousness*.

Chapter 2

1. Kuo-an was a Chinese Zen master in the 12th century.

2. Daisetsu Suzuki, *The Ten Oxherding Pictures: Manual of Zen Buddhism* (N.d., n.p.).

3. Pu-ming was a Chinese Zen master. Pu-ming's pictures can be seen in Spiegelman and Mokusen, *Buddhism and Jungian Psychology*, 104–8.

4. Shizuteru Ueda, "Emptiness and Fullness: Sunyata in Mahayana Buddhism," *The Eastern Buddhist* 15 (1982): 4–37.

5. Yuichi Kajiyama, "Bokugyuzu no Chibetto-ban ni

tsuite" ["On a Tibetan Version of Oxherding Pictures"] *Buk-kyo-shigaku* 7 (1958): 58–62.

6. Shizuteru Ueda and Seizan Yanagita, *Jugyuzu [Ten Oxherding Pictures]* (Tokyo: Chikuma Shobo, 1982).

7. Ibid.

8. Ibid.

9. Jung, "The Psychology of Transference," in *The Practice of Psychotherapy* in *Collected Works of Jung* 16: pp. 163–323.

10. J. Marvin Spiegelman, "The Oxherding Pictures of Zen Buddhism: A Commentary," in Spiegelman and Miyuki, *Buddhism and Jungian Psychology*, 43–87.

11. Neumann, *Origins and History of Consciousness*.

12. Shogo Kawahara, "Nazumi to sono kazoku" ["Nazumi and Her Family"], in *Futoko [School Refusal]*, ed. Sawako Suga (Kyoto, Japan: Jinbun Shoin, 1994), 21–54.

13. E. T. A. Hoffmann, *Der Goldne Topf [The Golden Pot]*, in *Collected Works*, by E. T. A. Hoffmann, Historical-Critical Edition, ed. Carl Georg von Maassen, vol. 1 (Leipzig, Germany: Univ. of Munich, 1912).

14. Hayao Kawai, *The Buddhist Priest Myoe: A Life of Dreams* (Venice, Calif.: Lapis Press, 1992).

15. Heisaku Kozawa, "Zaiakuishiki no Nishu" ["Two Kinds of Guilty Consciousness"], *Seishinbunseki-kenkyu* 1 (1954): 5–9.

16. Keigo Okonogi, "Ajase-Kompurekusu kara mita Nipponteki Taishokankei" ["Object Relations of the Japanese, in View of the *Ajase* Complex"], in Okonogi, *Moratorium Ningen no Jidai* (Tokyo: Chuo Koron Sha, 1978), 194–258.

17. Ibid.

18. Hayao Kawai, "The Transformation of Biblical Myths in Japan," *Diogenes* 42 (1994): 49–66.

19. Ma Satyam Savita, *Sagashite goran kimino ushi [Search for Your Own Bull]* (Kyoto, Japan: Zen Bunka Kenkyusho, 1987); in Japanese with English translation.

20. Kiyoshi Hiramatsu reported this case.

Chapter 3

1. Teru Takakura, *Indo dowa Shu [Fairy Tales of India]* (Tokyo: Ars Book Co., 1929), 161–65.

2. Sigmund Freud, *New Introductory Lectures on Psycho-Analysis*, trans. and ed. James Strachey (London: Hogarth Press, 1964), p. 80.

3. Bruno Bettelheim, *Freud and Man's Soul* (New York: Freeman Press, 1983).

4. *Konjaku Monogatari [Tales, Ancient and Modern]*, ed. Takao Yamada et al. 5 vols. (Tokyo: Iwanami Shoten, 1951).

5. William R. LaFleur, *The Karma of Words: Buddhism and the Literary Arts in Medieval Japan* (Berkeley: Univ. of California Press, 1983).

6. "Shinano no Kuni no Wato Kannon Shukke suru Koto" ["Wato Kannon in Shinano, Taking the Tonsure"], in *Konjaku Monogatari* 19, no. 11 (Tokyo: Iwanami Shoten), 87–89.

7. Jung, *Memories, Dreams, Reflections*, 323.

8. "Nishinokyo ni Taka o Tsukau Mono Yume o Mite Shukke suru Koto" ["A Hunter with Falcons Taking Tonsure by a Dream"], in *Konjaku Monogatari* 19, no. 8 (Tokyo: Iwanami Shoten), 77–80.

9. Adolph Guggenbuhl-Craig, *Power in the Helping Professions* (New York: Spring Publications, 1971).

10. Toshihiko Izutsu, "The Nexus of Ontological Events: A Buddhist View of Reality," in *Eranos Yearbook* 49 (1980) (Frankfurt am Main, Germany: Insel Verlag, 1981), 384–85.

11. Toshihiko Izutsu, *Cosmos to Anticosmos [Cosmos and Anticosmos]* (Tokyo: Iwanami Shoten, 1989), 18.

12. Ibid., 26.

13. Ibid., 41.

14. Jung, "On the Nature of the Psyche," in *Collected Works of Jung*, 8:217.

15. David H. Rosen, *Transforming Depression: A Jungian Approach Using The Creative Arts* (New York: G. P. Putnam's Sons, 1993).

Chapter 4

1. Jung, "Principles of Practical Psychotherapy," in *Collected Works of Jung*, 16:8.

2. Ibid.

3. Isao Kumakura, "Kata no genmitsusei to yuragi" ["Strictness and Swaying of *Kata*"], in *Kata to Nihonbunka*, ed. Minamoto Ryoen (Sobun Sha, 1992), 71–93.

4. Kawai, *Buddhist Priest Myoe*, 173–77.

5. *Collected Works of Jung*, 16:8.

6. Yoshito S. Hakeda, *The Awakening of Faith, Attributed to Asvaghosha* (New York: Columbia University Press, 1967).

7. Toshihiko Izutsu, *Ishiki-no Keijijogaku: Daijo-kishinron no Tetsugaku [Metaphysics of Consciousness: Philosophy of Awakening of the Faith in the Mahayana]* (Tokyo: Chuokoron-Sha, 1993).

8. Shizuteru Ueda, *Zen-Bukkyo [Zen Buddhism]* (Tokyo: Chikuma Shobo, 1973), 65.

9. Jung, "The Practical Use of Dream-Analysis," in *Collected Works of Jung*, 16:148.

10. Tomio Tada, *Meneki no Imiron [Semantics of Immunology]* (Tokyo: Seido Sha, 1993).

11. Dr. Marie-Louise von Franz recounted this episode in a lecture at the C. G. Jung Institute, Zurich, while I was a student there in 1962–65.

Epilogue

1. Jung, "Psychology of Transference," (1954): 172.

2. Shii Hae, trans. *A Thousand Winds [Sen no Kaze]* (Tokyo: Sango-Kan, 1995; English with Japanese translation).

Bibliography

Bettelheim, Bruno. *Freud and Man's Soul*. New York: Freeman Press, 1983.

Ellenberger, Henri F. *The Discovery of the Unconscious*. New York: Basic Books, 1970.

Freud, Sigmund. *New Introductory Lectures on Psycho-Analysis*, translated and edited by James Strachey. London: Hogarth Press, 1964.

Guggenbuhl-Craig, Adolf. *Power in the Helping Professions*. New York: Spring Publications, 1971.

Hakeda, Yoshito. *The Awakening of Faith, Attributed to Asvaghosha*. New York: Columbia University Press, 1967.

Herrigel, Eugen. *Zen and the Art of Archery*. New York: Pantheon Books, 1953.

Hoffmann, E. T. A. *Der Goldne Topf [The Golden Pot]*. In *Collected Works*, by E. T. A. Hoffmann. Historical-Critical Edition, edited by Carl Georg von Maassen. Vol. 1. Leipzig, Germany: University of Munich, 1912; in German.

Izutsu, Toshihiko. *Cosmos to Anticosmos [Cosmos and Anticosmos]*. Tokyo: Iwanami Shoten, 1989; in Japanese.

————. *Ishiki-no Keijijogaku: Daijo-kishi-ron no Tetsugaku [Metaphysics of Consciousness: Philosophy of Awakening of Faith]*. Tokyo: Chuokoron-shya, 1993; in Japanese.

————. "The Nexus of Ontological Events: A Buddhist View of Reality." *Eranos Yearbook* 49 (1980). Frankfurt am Main, Germany: Insel Verlag, 1981.

————. *Toward a Philosophy of Zen Buddhism.* Tehran: Imperial Iranian Academy of Philosophy, 1977.

Jung, C. G. *The Collected Works of C. G. Jung,* edited by H. Read, M. Fordam, and G. Adler. Princeton, N.J.: Princeton University Press, 1953–79.

————. Foreword to *Introduction to Zen Buddhism,* by Daisetsu T. Suzuki. New York: Doubleday, 1956. Reprinted in *Psychology and Religion: East and West,* 2d ed., and in *Collected Works of C. G. Jung,* ed. H. Read, M. Fordam, and G. Adler.

————. *Memories, Dreams, Reflections,* edited by Aniela Jaffe. London: Collins and Routledge and Kegan Paul, 1963.

Kajiyama, Yuichi. "Bokugyuzu no Chibetto-ban ni tsuite" ["On a Tibetan Version of Oxherding Pictures"]. *Bukkyoshigaku* 7, no. 3; in Japanese.

Kawahara, Shogo. "Nazumi to sono kazoku" ["Nazumi and Her Family"]. In *Futoko [School Refusal],* edited by Sawako Suga. Kyoto, Japan: Jinbun Shoin, 1984; in Japanese.

Kawai, Hayao. *The Buddhist Priest Myoe: A Life of Dreams.* Venice, Calif.: Lapis Press, 1992.

————. *Dreams, Myths and Fairy Tales in Japan.* Einsiedeln, Switzerland: Daimon, 1995.

————. "Genkei to shiet no Ro-nyaku dan-jo" [Old, Young, Male, and Female as Archetypes"]. In *Ro-nyaku no Jiku, Danjo no Jiku,* edited by Kenzaburo Oe et al. Tokyo: Iwanami Shoten, 1951; in Japanese.

————. *The Japanese Psyche: Major Motifs in the Fairy Tales of Japan.* Dallas: Spring Publications, 1988).

————. "The Transformation of Biblical Myths in Japan." In *Diogenes* 42, no. 165. International Council of Philosophy and Humanistic Studies, 1994.

Konjaku Monogatari [Tales, Ancient and Modern]. Tokyo: Iwanami Shoten, 1951; in Japanese.

Kozawa, Heisaku. "Zaiakuishiki no Nishu" ["Two Kinds of Guilty Consciousness"]. *Seishinbunseki-kenkyu*, 1954; in Japanese.

Kumakura, Isao. "Kata no genmitsusei to yuragi" ["Strictness and Swaying of *Kata*"]. In *Kata to Nihonbunka*, edited by Minamoto Ryoen. Tokyo: Sobun Sha, 1992; in Japanese.

LaFleur, William R. *The Karma of Words: Buddhism and the Literary Arts in Medieval Japan*. Berkeley: University of California Press, 1983.

Miyuki, Mokusen. "A Jungian Approach to the Pure Land Practice of Nien-fo." *Journal of Analytical Psychology* 25, no. 3 (1980): 265–74.

Neumann, Erich. *The Origins and History of Consciousness*. New York: Bollingen Foundation and Pantheon Books, 1954.

Okonogi, Keigo. "Der Ajase-Komplex des Japaners" ["The Ajase-Complex of Japanese"]. In *Die Kuele Seele Selbstinterpretationen der japanischen Kultur*, edited by Jens Heise. Frankfurt am Main: Fischer Taschenbuch Verlag, 1990; in German.

———. "Ajase-Kompurekusu kara mita Nipponteki Taishokankei" ["Object Relations of the Japanese, in View of the *Ajase* Complex"]. *Moratorium Ningen no Jidai*. Tokyo: Chuo Koron Sha, 1978; in Japanese.

Savita, Ma Satyam. *Sagashite goran kimino ushi [Search for Your Own Bull]*. Kyoto, Japan: Zen Bunka Kenkyusho, 1987; in Japanese.

Shibayama, Zenkei, and Gyokusei Jikihara. *Zen no Bokugyuzu [Oxherding Pictures of Zen]*. Osaka, Japan: Sogen Sha, 1967; in Japanese.

Spiegelman, J. Marvin, and Mokusen Miyuki. *Buddhism and Jungian Psychology*. Phoenix, Ariz.: Falcon Press, 1985.

Suzuki, Daisetsu T. *The Ten Oxherding Pictures: Manual of Zen Buddhism*. No publisher, no date.

———. *Zen Buddhism*. New York: Doubleday, 1956.

Rosen, H. David. *Transforming Depression: A Jungian Approach Using The Creative Arts*. New York: G. P. Putnam's Sons, 1993.

Tada, Tomio. *Meneki no Imiron [Semantics of Immunology]*. Tokyo: Seido Sha, 1993; in Japanese.

Takakura, Teru. *Indo dowa Shu [Fairy Tales of India]*. Ars Book Co., 1929; in Japanese.

Ueda, Shizuteru. "Ascent and Descent: Zen Buddhism in Comparison with Meister Eckhart." *The Eastern Buddhist* 16 (1983): 52–72.

———. "Emptiness and Fullness: Sunyata in Mahayana Buddhism." In *The Eastern Buddhist* 15 (1982): 9–37.

———. *Zen-Bukkyo [Zen Buddhism]*. Tokyo: Chikuma Shobo, 1973; in Japanese.

Ueda, Shizuteru, and Seizan Yanagita. *Jugyuzu [Ten Oxherding Pictures]*. Tokyo: Chikuma Shobo, 1982; in Japanese.

Index